BRAHMANICAL GODS IN BURMA

BRAHMANICAL GODS IN BURMA

Indian Art and Iconography

By

Nihar-Ranjan Ray

BKP

BHARATIYA KALA PRAKASHAN

Delhi : : (India)

First Edition : 1927
Revised Edition : 2010

Published by **C.P. Gautam**
BHARATIYA KALA PRAKASHAN
3421-A, IInd Floor, Narang Colony, Tri Nagar,
Delhi-110035. Telefax : 27393083, Phone : 32967505
E-mail : bkp3421@yahoo.co.in
Website : www.bkpbooks.com

ISBN : 978-81-8090-256-7

Laser Type Setting
Creative Graphics

Printed by :
G.S. Offset Printers
Delhi

Contents

Preface

This monograph is an outcome of my studies and researches in the domain of Burmese Art, Archaeology and History that I have been pursuing for the last four years. My original subject was, and still is, a comprehensive study of the origin and history of Architecters in Burma—an almost untrodden field of study and reserch, but one that is gradually yielding results that would contribute, I hope, considerably to our advancement of knowledge of a very important aspect of early Indo-Burmese relations. In course of my studies and investigations on the spot in that connection, I was struck by the presence of a considerable number of Brahmanical images scattered all over the Peninsula interesting from both artistic as well as iconographic points of view. Professedly Buddhistic as Burma was from very early times, and still is, these images very naturally invited my attention, and a close preliminary observation convinced me that systematic iconographic and artistic study of them would be much help to my further studies in this field, especially in the study of Burmese monuments. Accordingly, I took it up, and here I put forward the record of my work.

Both geographically and culturally Burma is a projection of the Indian continent, and formed a part of Indo-China and ancient Campa, Kamboj and Siam-Laos. Attention of scholars as well as of laymen has been drawn to the subject of Indian colonial enterprise in the past in those countries as well as in the island colonies of Java and Sumatra, Bali and Barneo where important archaeological discoveries have been made during the last twenty-five years by French and Dutch scholars. But, unfortunately indeed, the same cannot equally be said of Burma; the amount of attention of Eastern and Western scholars, the study of the history and archaeology of this less-introductory know the Indian Orient is not what it ought to have been. In fact, archaeological study and investigation in Burma is a thing of recent devolopment; and whatever the Archaeological Department of Burma has done in the domain of Early Burmese History and Geography, Art and Archaeology, Iconography and Religion, and above all Epigraphy, during the last three decades in mainly the work of one man, Mon. Charles Duroiselle, lately Superintendent, Archaeological Survey, Burma. And, whosoever has worked or attempted to work, in the domain of Burmese History and Archaeology in recent years must, first of all, recognise and acknowledge with gratitude, as I do here, the researches carried out by him and his Department. To him, therefore, I dedicate this humble piece of work.

But, inspite of the valuable work he and his Department have done, the images studied and described in the following pages have not yet received their due recognition. No systematic study to bring out fully their iconographic significance and their learning upon ealry Indo-Burmese historical and cultural relations have yet been pursued. Most of them have not even been identified and some had even to be rediscovered from the *debris* of finds thing ago made. I, therefore, make no apalogy in presenting for one first time a detailed analytical study of these Brahmanical sages in all their bearings as the subject of a short monograph.

A careful perusal of these pages would show that my hopes have more than justified themselves, and that I have been able, many claim, to obtain results than would enable us to have a clearer understanding at least of one aspect of early Indo-Burmese relations. Moreover, any one interested in Indian Iconography would be able to find in these imges that are described and illustrated here new types and variations till now unknown, as also remarkable affinities with those that are more or less familiar to us. In both cases, a really interested mind has much to take delight in.

The materials of this monograph were collected by me during by the archaeological tours that I had made throughout Burma in 1927 and 1929. In this connection I must record any sense of gratitude to Prof. B.M. Barua, M.A., D.Litt. (London), whodrew my attention to the study of Burmology, to Dr. D.R. Bhandarkar, Carmichael Professor of Ancient Indian History and Culture, Calcutta University, who guided me with care and interest through my studies, and to my teachers in the Post-Graduate Department of the Calcutta University for their kind encouragement. To Mr. K.N. Dikshit, M.A., lately Deputy Director General for Explorations, Archaeological Survey of India, I am under a debt of gratitude for his kindly going through the entire manuscript and encouraging me in my Burmese studies and researchers. I would certainly fail in my duty if I do not record here my obligation to the Archaeological Survey Department of India and Burma but for whose kindness and courtesy the illustrations which are so indispensable for an intelligent understanding of the subject could not have been published. I am to thank my wife, Srimati Manika Devi, B.A., for kindly preparing the Index. I should also acknowledge with sincere thanks the very kind interest Mr. J.C. Chakravorti, M.A., Assistant Registrar, Calcutta University, and Mr. A.C. Ghatak, M.A., Superintendent, with his staff of the Calcutta University Press, have taken in the publication of my humble work.

Nihar-Ranjan Ray

List of Illustrations

century A.D. (Courtesy: Archaeological Survey, Burma).

Pl. 16 *Kalki avatāra* of *Viṣṇu;* in an outer niche of the *Nāt hlaung* temple, Pagan: portions of the body badly mutilated. C. 10th-11th century A.D. (Courtesy: Archaeological Survey, Burma).

Pl. 17 Four-handed *Viṣṇu* standing on lotus pedestal; originally discovered at Myinkaba, now in the Ananda Museum, Pagan: bronze, well-preserved. C. 13th-14th century A.D. (Courtesy: Archaeological Survey, Burma).

Pl. 18 Śaivite coins bearing obverse and reverse legends of bull and trident respectively, belonging to the ancient *Candra* dynasty of kings of Arakan; inscribed in *nāgarī* characters of the 9th-11th century A.D. (Phayre: Coins of Arakan, Pegu and Burma, Plate II, nos. 1, 4, 8; pp. 28-29).

Pl. 19 Coins bearing obverse and reverse legends of *Viṣṇuite* conch-shell and Śaivite trident respectively, belonging probably to the ancient *Candra* dynasty of kings of Arakan. (Phayre : Coins of Arakan, Pegu and Burma, plate V, nos. 6 and 7 and plate II, no. 10; p. 33 and p. 29).

Pl. 20 *Śiva* and *Pārvatī* seated: originally discovered at Thātoñ now in the Government Museum, Rangoon: well preserved, though slightly mutilated. C. 9th century A.D. (Courtesy Archaeological Survey, Burma).

Pl. 21 *Śiva* standing: originally discovered amidst the debris of ruins within the *Nāt-hlaung* temple, Pagan; now in the Ananda Museum: well preserved. C. 13th century A.D. (Courtesy : Archaeological Survey, Burma).

Pl. 22 *Śiva* seated in *rāja-līlā :* originally discovered near *Shwe-ōnhmin* monastery at Myinpagan; now in the Ananda Museum, Pagan: very badly mutilated. C.

10th-11th century A.D. (Courtesy : Archaeological Survey, Burma).

Pl. 23 *Devī* slaying the *Mahiṣāsura* (buffalo-demon); originally discovered at Wesali, Arakan; now at the office of the Honorary Archaeological Officer, Arakan : upper portion and sides of slab entirely broken off, very badly corroded. *C.* 6th-7th century A.D. (Courtesy: Archaeological Survey, Burma).

Pl. 24 *Sūrya* driving a chariot drawn by seven horses originally discovered at Mrohaung, Arakan; now at the office of the Honorary Archaeological Officer, Arakan : very badly mutilated. *C.* 6th 7th century A.D. (Courtesy: Archaeological Survey, Burma).

Pl. 25 *Gaṇeśa* seated in *padmāsana,* Ananda Museum, Pagan : very badly mutilated. *C.* 11th-12th century A.D. (Courtesy: Archaeological Survey, Burma).

Pl. 26 *Gaṇeśa* seated in *padmāsana,* Ananda Museum, Pagan : very badly weathered. *C.* 12th-13th century A.D. (Courtesy: Archaeological Survey, Burma).

Pl. 27 *Gaṇeśa* seated on a pedestal showing on its fate a crocodile, and on the right and left a tortoise and a fish respectively: originally found at Pagan; now at the office of the Archaeological Survey, Mandalay: good state of preservation. *C.* 13th-14th century A.D. (Courtesy: Archaeological Survey, Burma).

Pl. 28 *Brahmā* seated in *padmāsana,* Ananda Museum, Pagan: portions of the body, broken off. *C.* 9th-10th century A.D. (Courtesy: Archaeological Survey, Burma).

Pl. 29 *Brahmā* seated in *padmāsana,* Government Museum, Rangoon: well-preserved. *C.* 12th century A.D. (Courtesy: Archaeological Survey, Burma).

Pl. 30 *Brahmā* seated in *līlāsana, Nanpaya* temple, Myinpagan, Pagan; very well-preserved. *C.* 11th century A.D. (Courtesy: Archaeological Survey, Burma).

1 Introductory

Burma is professedly Buddhist and follows the Pāli Canon of the Southern School. The story of the introduction of Buddhism into Pagan in Upper Burma is well-known. It occurred in the third quarter of the 11th century A.D., when Pagan was fast rising into importance. There is no settled system of chronology before this, and systematic historical records are completely lacking with the exception of a few important events which folk-memory had taken care to preserve in native chronicles. The earliest epigraphic records found in Burma hail from Hmawza, a village five miles south of Prome, and, no doubt, date back to an earlier period, probably to the 5th or 6th century A.D., but no definite sequence of historical events can be reconstructed from them. As far as our present knowledge goes, early Burmese history has its beginnings at a time when we are in the thick of the medieval period of Indian history, and we are immediately introduced to a powerful dynasty of kings—zealous patrons and devoted followers of an Indian faith, the Southern Buddhism of the Pāli Canon—ruling at Pagan. A Talaing monk of the *Theravāda* School of Buddhism and an inhabitant of Thātoñ in *Ramaññadeśa* leltaic Burma), Shin Arahan, came over to Pagan in 1056 A.D., and lived there in a solitary corner of the citadel when he day, so the story goes, be was taken to the Court. He treated a great impression on the king with his yellow robe, this sublime purity of life and lofty graciousness of speech. The king of Pagan, Anawrahta asked: 'Master, of what race art thou? Whence comest thou? Whose doctrine dost thou follow?' Shin Arahan told him, and

Anawrahta entreated him saying, 'My Lord, teach me somewhat, yea, though it be a little, of the religion preached by the Lord, the Master.' Before long, the apostle's first step was accomplished, he had won authority to his side. But Shin Arahan had brought no sacred books, for writing was still a rare gift. His mission could not thrive without them and he urged Anawrahta to procure copies from Thātoñ where there were thirty complete sets of the *Tripiṭaka,* the Three Scriptures. Envoys were sent but returned with art insulting refusal. Stung to anger Anawrahta marched on Thātoñ with all his men."[1]

At the end of a long siege Thātoñ ceased to be a royal city, and the victorious king of Pagan returned to the capital with the most valuable treasures of the Faith, a host of Buddhist monks, and with them thirty-two white elephants each laden with scriptures and relics, all belonging to Manuha, the Talaing king of Thātoñ. Thātoñ was annexed and Manuha kept a captive in Pagan; but, as has so often happened in history, the culture of the vanquished predominated over that of the victors, and the Southern Buddhism of Thātoñ gradually spread throughout Upper Burma.

The question now arises : when did Thātoñ, or more properly *Rammaññadeśa,* the land *par excellence* of the Talaings, adopt the faith of *Theravāda* Buddhism, *i.e.,* Buddhism of the *Hīnayāna* form? Are we to accept the tradition–so insistent in Burmese records—of the Aśoka-mission of Sona and Uttara to *Suvaṇṇabhūmi,* or should we rely upon the later tradition that Buddhaghoṣa, the celebrated Buddhist encyclopaedist, crossed over the Burma and preached there the religion of the Master? Available evidence is so meagre that the question cannot be answered satisfactorily, and recent criticism has thrown doubt on both the treaditions. It is equally difficult to determine whether the religion was first introduced from Ceylon or from some other country. The only thing which can be asserted with certainty at this stage of historical research is that the introduction of the Faith must have taken place not later than the 5th or 6th century A.D., but the actual circumstances are totally unknown to us. The earliest epigraphic records found in Burma hail not from Thātoñ, but from Hmawza, or old Prome. They comprise up to date two gold plates discovered at Maunggan, a village near Hmawza, two fragments of a stone inscription found at the Bawbawgyi pagoda, a line of inscription around the rim of the top of the cover of a small votive *Stūpa* discovered at Hmawza, and finally a manuscript containing twenty gold leaves each inscribed on one side placed within two covers of the same metal. The Maunggan plates begin each with the well-known Buddhist formula : *Ye dhammā,* etc., which is followed by 19 categories from the *Abhidhamma* in numerical order, and lastly by the well-known praise of the *Triratna.* Mon. Finot's remarks on them are most valuable. "The language is Pāli. The script has a very archaic aspect; it reminds one of the *Kadamba* script of the 5th century A.D. We cannot be far out of the 6th or 7th century of the Christian era. It is interesting to find the Pāli canon in use in Lower Burma at so ancient a period when the rest of Further India was acquainted with *Mahāyāna* Buddhism and its Sanskrit text." The fragmentary stone inscription contains an extract from the *Vibhaṅga,* a book of the *Abhidhamma.* The golden-leaf manuscript, however, contains extracts from the *Abhidhamma* and *Vinaya Piṭakas.* The language of all these epigraphic records is Pāli, and the writing is, in all these instances, in character of an early South Indian script of the Canara-Telegu type.' They can thus safely be assigned to the 5th and 6th centuries of the Christian era.[2] *Hīnayāna* Buddhism, thus, must have been known in Lower Burma at least four centuries before it came to be introduced in Pagan, at a time which marked the growth of a great *Hīnayāna* movement in India with its centre at Conjeeveram or ancient *Kāñchīpuram* on the Madras coast.

But, wherefrom did this Pāli Buddhism first come to Burma? So long as the possibility of the penetration of early North Indian Hinayanism (as distinct from later Pāli Buddhism of the South) into Burma directly from the North is not finally disposed of, it cannot be asserted that Burma originally received her Faith from Ceylon. It is true that the Buddhism of Thātoñ (Lower Burma) as well as of Pagan was of the Ceylonese form; but the earliest Pāli inscriptions found at Hmawza, just referred to, though unmistakably Buddhist in character, do riot exclusively refer to the Ceylonese School of Pāli Buddhism. In Pagan, the case seems to have been otherwise. Tradition as well as native chronicles point to the middle of the 11th century as the time when Pāli was introduced there along with Ceylonese Buddhism. But recent discoveries have proved that Sanskrit was known in the royal capital some centuries earlier, 'at least as the language of the Indian court-astronomers, and perhaps also as the classical language of the *Southern Buddhist sect whose canon was sanskritic.*' (An. Rep. A. S. India, 1926-27, pp. 161ff.) Furthermore, it is now almost certain that there was a strong infiltration of Hinduised Mahayanism in Pagan directly from North-east India at an early period.[3] It may not, however, be impossible, therefore, that a still earlier stratum of Hinayanism of the Northern School had been lying dormant until a vigorous revival was caused by the later penetration of the Southern School of Pāli Buddhism from Ceylon, first in Lower Burma and then, by the 11th century, in Pagan in Upper Burma. But this must remain a tentative suggestion only until it is definitely proved or rejected.

This is all that we know and can guess regarding the introduction of Buddhism in Burma. We must now turn to a more interesting question : how far did Brahmanism penetrate Burma ?

We know that in South-east Asia almost all the countries that had been colonized by Indians or had close commercial contact with India were permeated with Brahmanical culture and its elaborate paraphernalia of rites and rituals, gods and goddesses, and myths and legends. In Java, where the *Śailendras* of *Śrīvijaya* were a Buddhist dynasty and where Buddhism (no doubt of the *Mahāyāna* form) had the strongest hold, Brahmanism hardly acknowledged a less important position. The two religions flourished side by side, and if Buddhism with its clergy and laity and rules of conduct became dominant, Brahmanism with its gods and goddesses, and rites and rituals did not however, suffer in popularity. In Campa, as well as in Kamboj, it was Brahmanism that had the larger following; the royal dynasties were mostly Brahmanical, and the gods of the Buddhist pantheon had but few followers. In Siam, which like Burma is professedly Buddhist, finds of Brahmanical deities, in considerable numbers testify to the existence of a large Brahmanical population. It, therefore, appears unlikely that Burma alone escaped all traces of Brahmanical influence.

In fact, Indian elements are found in profusion in the early *Mōn* inscriptions of B Brahma. The use of Sanskritic religious terms (*e.g., Svar* for *Svarga, Dharma,* etc.), royal names and styles, and certain religious and social observances occur frequently, but they are common to both Brahmanism and Sanskritic Buddhism. As to the use of Sanskrit terms too, it may be urged that a form of Buddhism using Sanskrit as its sacred language had probably existed in Burma from early times. Even making all such allowances there are strong reasons for believing that Brahmanism had its share of responsibility for the strong Sanskritic element present in the early *Mōn* records.[4] The numerous references to *Brāhmaṇas* in these records show their great influence in the Buddhist courts. Rituals and ceremonies performed, by them are partly Brahmanical in character, and the god who is invariably worshipped has been identified as *Nārāyaṇa-Viṣṇu.*[5] We also have the story of one of the most celebrated kings of the Pagan dynasty—Kyanzittha was his name—who in one of his former births was once a *Viṣṇu,* and on another occasion was born in the family of *Rāma,* king of Oudh.[6] This legend has an unique interest inasmuch as it shows a distinct blending of the Buddhist theory of re-birth with purely Brahmanical legends. It is no less remarkable that in the same records we find mention of the "four castes" who are directed to perform their respective duties.

"A remarkable proportion of loan words in these records is of Sanskrit origin, not Pāli ......As to the reason for their presence in early *Mōn,* allowance must be made for the fact that *Brāhmaṇas,* who are often mentioned in the inscriptions, played a great part at all the Indo-Chinese courts, from Burma to Campa. Vestiges of Hinduism have been found in Lower Burma, though they are not so common as in several other parts of Indo-China. But there is much reason to believe that some form of Buddhism using Sanskrit as its sacred language also existed there in former times, just as it did, for example, in Kamboj .....The soundest inference seems to be the one drawn by Finōt that Sanskrit and Pāli (and the several forms of religion with which they are respectively associated) were more or less concurrent influences in the *Mōn* country from an early period. Whatever may have been the channel or channels through which Sanskrit words came in, they are present in such numbers that the strength of the influences that introduced them must have been considerable and probably extended over a fairly long period." (Ep. Birminica, Vol. I, Part II, p. 76.)

To have an idea of the strong Brahmanical element in

the *Mōn* inscriptions, we shall here quote only a few selected passages from the records already referred to. *Mōn* Inscriptions No. IX (found near the *Tharaba* gate, Pagan)[7] has the following passage :

"The *Brāhmaṇa* astrologers went (and) drew water and (bathed), the side pillars, the *yas* pillars, the *atas* pillars, etc., etc. ....(At) All these seventeen places, they made a decoration of plantains, adorned with young plantains, (and) sugar cane (and set?) water (in) vessels of gold (and), silver (and) water (in) conch-shells wherein (they) put cleaned rice (and) *dubbā* grass (and) spread mats (with) golden flowers, altar oblations and altar candles. Having (arranged them?); they made in honour of *Nārāyaṇa,* decoration of plantains ...... then the *Brāhmaṇa* astrologers worshipped *Nārāyaṇa.*"[8]

We notice here the characterisically Brahmanical ritual of using plantain trees as well as *dubbā* grass in a religious ceremony.

"At the auspicious time .....*godhūli* (being) *lagna,* the expert *Brāhmaṇa* astrologers bathed the side pillars, etc....[9]

An essentially Brahmanical custom was made use of in a Buddhist coronation ceremonial presided over by *Brāhmaṇa* priests when the different pillars referred to above were bound by sacred Brahmanical threads in a hundred and eight spools.

"The thread wherewith they bound up the pillars, tender maidens, young damsels, daughters of *Brāhmaṇas,* had spun (it and) made (it on) *a hundred and eight spools*. Then the *Brāhmaṇa* astrologers recited and sprinkled water and after that they bound up the pillars."[10]

These and numerous other similar references clearly indicate the existence of a considerable number of *Brāhmaṇas* in Burmese courts as priests, astrologers, and experts in housebuilding, who must have occupied positions of influence and importance there. And not only were there the *Brāhmaṇas,* the other three castes as well of the Brahmanical fold were there. Thus we read the pious wish of a pious king :

"All the monks shall be full of virtue and good conduct. All the *Brāhmaṇas,* who know the *Vedas,* they shall fulfill all the *Brāhmaṇa* Law. All the princes shall carry out the Law altogether. The 'four castes ' shall fulfill their Law also."[10]

Brahmanism was not the religion of the State nor of the people in general, but the records referred to above seem to show that there was a considerable number of followers of the Brahmanical religion, not exclusively *Brāhmaṇas,* but of other three castes as well, who were free to perform their own religious ceremonies., Brahmanical influence is also indicated by certain ancient place names[12] of both Upper and Lower Burma. Such a name is *Bissunomyo,* which is equivalent to *Viṣṇupura* or the city of *Viṣṇu.* The name was in ancient times applied to old Prome or Hmawza which had obviously been a centre of Viṣṇuite influences. The tradition of the foundation of the ancient city of Prome as contained in the *Mahayazawin,* a late Burmese chronicle, is associated with *Viṣṇu* and and his *vāhana, Garuḍa,* as also with *Caṇḍī* and *Parameśvara* equivalent to *Durgā* and *Śiva* respectively.[13] The *Mahayazawin* does not mention the name of *Viṣṇu* but refers to a Ṛṣi. The name of the Ṛṣi is supplied by the great *Shwezigōn* inscription[14] which records briefly the story of the foundation of *Sisit* (or old Prome). Old Prome or Hmawza is also referred to as *Śrī Kṣetra* (mentioned in early *Mōn* records, as *Sisit* or *Srikṣet)* which is the sacred name of modern Purī on the opposite side of the Bay of Bengal, and is associated with a strong Brahmanical tradition. Taungdwin, a town, said to have been founded in 837 A.D., was called *Rāmāvatī* after the name of the epic hero, *Rāma,* who is recognised as one of the ten incarnations of *Viṣṇu.*

But the surest proof of the prevalence of Brahmanism in Burma is the archaeological discoveries of Brahmanical gods and temples. Of such discoveries we have, though not at all comparable with other parts of South-east Asia; an interesting record. Of Hindu temples in ancient Burma, we have only one, the *Nat-hlaung kyaung* that stand at Pagan. The main deity of the shrine is *Viṣṇu* himself, four images of whom stand on the four sides of a square obelisk at the centre of the vaulted temple. Its walls and niches are adorned with stone images of the ten principal and other subsidiary incarnations of the main deity.[15] This temple is most probably referred to in a Tamil inscription found at Myinpagan, belonging paleographically to the 12th century A.D., and purporting to record " gifts by a native of *Magodayar pattanam* in *Malaimaṇḍalam, i.e.,* Cranganore in Malabar, His name *Śrī Kulaśekhara-nambi* stamps him as a devotee of the *Vaisnava* saint *Kulaśekhara* from whose *Mukundamālā* the opening verse (of the inscription) is derived. The recipient of the gift was the *Viṣṇu* temple of *Nānādeśī Vinnagara* at *Pukkam* alias *Arivattanapura,* i.e., Pagan.... *Nānādeśī Vinnagara* means the *Viṣṇu* temple of those coming from various countries. This name shows that the temple, which was situated in the heart of the Buddhist country of Burma, had been founded and was resorted to by *Vaiṣṇavas* from various parts of the Indian Peninsula.[16]

The existence of a Brahmanical population (mainly Vaiṣṇavite in creed) in Burma at an early period cannot, therefore, be doubted. It can easily be surmised that this Brahmanical community would have their own gods whom they could worship in accordance with their own religious rites. In those localities where the Indian element was permanently represented either by a more vigorous commercial intercourse or by settlement and colonization, it was likely that their gods would have permanent habitats there in temples. These temples having been usually built of brick gradually fell into decay aid finally disappeared with the singular exception of the one that is now standing at Pagan. But, most of the images which had been once enshrined in these temples are now emerging out of the dēbris of ruins of centuries. Thus, at old Hmawza, a locality known in ancient times as *Bissunamyo*, at least three different types of stone images of *Viṣṇu* have been discovered, one of which belongs to the 6th or 7th century A.D.,[17] along with images of *Gaṇeśa, Brahmā* and other Brahmanical deities. At Mergui in the Tennasserim province images of *Viṣṇu, Gaṇeśa, Hanumāna* and *Brahmā* have been found.[18] Three stone slabs, belonging stylistically to about the latter half of the 9th century A.D., have in recent years been brought over from Thātoñ to the Rangoon Museum. Two of these slabs depict in bold relief the *Ānanta-śayyā* episode of *Viṣṇu* and the third represents *Śiva* with *Pārvatī* seated by his side.[19] At Thātoñ, the walls of a pyramidal stage of a Buddhist pagoda are decorated with rectangular stone panels purporting probably to depict a Hindu mythological story. Of the slabs that still remain, two certainly represent *Śiva* with his trident. In Arakan where Brahmanical influence had been more pronounced from earlier times, archaeological exploration has discovered in recent years images of *Viṣṇu, Durgā, Sūrya* and other Hindu deities. Of these, the image of *Durgā*[20] and *Sūrya*[21] undoubtedly belong to the late Gupta period, and can in no way be dated later than the 8th century A.D. Coins and terracotta tablets bearing the Śaivite symbol of the trident and the representation of the bull *Nandī* have been found in large numbers at Mrohaung and other localities in Arakan as well as in other places of both Upper and Lower Burma. Coins with the Vaiṣṇavite symbol of a conch-shell are not also infrequent.

The above references do not by any means exhaust the

list of finds of Brahmanical gods and articles of worship in Burma. But these even are sufficient to make us realise that they deserve a careful study. And such a study would throw a great deal of light on certain fundamental problems in the history of Indo-Burmese historical and cultural relations in early times. A detailed stylistic comparison with similar images in India would enable us to determine approximately the age in which historical relations between India and Burma became definitely established, and also the period during which the Brahmanical element came and continued to exert an appreciable influence in the Peninsula. It would also indicate from which part or parts of India the Indian colonists of Burma were derived.

A comparative study of Brahmanical influence in Burma and in other countries of South-east Asia has a still wider interest. We may notice here one or two points in this connexion. Finds of Brahmanical gods in Burma are much less important both in numbers and types, when compared to similar finds in other sister colonies of the Indian Orient. The natural inference would be that Brahmanism played a less significant part in the life of the people in Burma. It is true that certain traces of Brahmanical rites and rituals and myths and traditions had come to be interwoven into the texture of the social and religious life of the country. The attitude of the court as well as of the people towards the Brahmanical population and their gods was one of utmost religious toleration (otherwise Hindu temples could never have been erected), and Brahmanism was allowed to exist side by side with Buddhism which had an overwhelming following, and was the religion of the State and of the people; Naturally enough, the followers of the latter religion did not altogether escape from the influence of the former. Yet it must be recognised that this influence remained mainly superficial and did hardly affect the cultural life of the people at large.

Why did Brahmanism fail to exert a stronger influence and touch the soul of the people deeper in Burma, as it had succeeded in doing in Java or Sumatra, or in other parts of Indo-China, for example, in Campa and Kamboj? Here it is only possible to suggest a tentative suggestion for consideration. It should be remembered that everywhere in the Indian colonies in the South-east, with the one exception of Burma, it was the Northern or *Mahāyāna* form of Buddhism that had any following. It should also be remembered that *Mahāyāna* Buddhism in its ceremonial aspect and in its attitude towards gods and deities had great affinities with Brahmanism. Both had a multitude of gods and goddesses and in certain ritualistic aspects they differed but little. It is this resemblance which made it possible for Brahmanism to exert a powerful influence on the followers of the *Mahāyāna* form of Buddhism. The gods belonging to both could mix freely as the two pantheons were not separated by any marked difference in principle or practice. The *Hīnayāna* form, on the other hand, had no pantheon at all, and it was definitely opposed to the very idea of gods and goddesses. This made it impossible for Hinayanism to accommodate Brahmanism within its fold. In Burma it tolerated Brahmanical rituals and ceremonials presided over by *Brāhmaṇa* priests, but never allowed Brahmanical gods to trespass within its own sacred precincts. Burma was not thus a congenial soil for the propagation of the Brahmanical faith. One indirect result was that there were no new converts into Brahmanism, so that the Brahmanical population remained a separate and isolated community from the very beginning, and was tolerated as such by the much more numerous Buddhist population.

This, however, does not minimise the importance of the study of the Brahmanical gods in Burma. Apart from the historical interest, a close study is likely to furnish types and forms that are at present unknown in Indian Iconography, which are unique local renderings of Indian originals and which give expression to new artistic impulses independent of orthodox traditions, or which follow a different set of artistic canons yet unknown to us. In any case, such a study is certain to advance our knowledge of Indian Art and Iconography.

REFERENCES

1. Harvey, *History of Burma*, pp. 26-28.
2. Finōt, *Jour. Asiatique*, Vol. XX, 1912, pp. 121ff-; *An. Rep.* A. S. Burma, 1909-10; Duroiselle. An. Rep. A. S. Burma, 1924, pp. 2122; An. Rep. A. S. India, 1926-27, pp. 171ff.
3. The existence of Mahayanism and Mahayanist Tantrikism in Upper Burma before the introduction of Pāli Buddhism from Thātoñ has been definitely established by the discovery of some stone and bronze images of *Mahāyāna* gods *(Avalokiteśvara, Tārā, Maitreya,* etc.) and by the existence of the *Aris,* a Tantrik Buddhist sect belonging to the Northern School. (Duroiselle, The *Aris* of Burma and Tantric Buddhism, An. Rep. A.S. Ind., 1915-16.)

   This is confirmed by Tibetan texts as also by the evidence of Tārānātha and by the wall-paintings of the *Payathonzu* and *Nandamañña* temples of Minnanthu in Pagan. Mention of the Mahayanist god *Lokeśvara* along with *Maitreya is* frequently made in Talaing, Sanskrit and Burmese records. The cult of Bodhisattva *Lokanātha* seems also to have been very widely known; images of *Lokanātha* have, in fact, been discovered in Pagan. And, I think, I have been able to discover a life-like standing image of the same divinity accompanied by *Tārā* and *Hayagrīva* represented in line and colour on the right wall of the entrance vestibule of the Kyaubaukkyi Pagoda, Pagan. Stone and bronze images of Bodhisattvas have from time to time been discovered at Pagan and old Prome.
4. Blagden, *Ep. Birminica,* Vol. I, Part II, p. 76. Indian Element in the Inscriptions.
5. Ep. Birminica, Vol. III, Part I.
6. *Ibid.,* Vol. I, Part II, Mon. Insc. Nos. I and III.
7. *Ibid.,* Vol. III, Part I.
8. *Ibid.,* pp. 42-43.
9. *Ibid,* p. 36.

10. *Ibid.*, pp. 50-51.
11. Ep. Birminica, Vol. I, Part II, Mon. Insc. No. I, Sec. G., p. 127. But regarding the mention of 'four castes,' Prof. Blagden is, however, of opinion that this is a merely conventional phrase used to denote "people in general." "There is no reason," he says, "to believe that apart from *Brāhmaṇas* who were of foreign introduction, any real division into castes was recognised " (p. 75).
12. Duroiselle, Apocryphal Geography of Burma, *An. Rep. A. S. Burma*, 1923, p. 15.
13. An. Rep. A. S. Burma, 1910, p. 18.
14. Ep. Birm., Vol. I, Part II, p. 90.
15. An. Rep. A.S. India, 1212-13.
16. Hultzsch. An. Rep. A.S. Burma, 1902-3, p. 7.
17. Phongyi Kyaung Museum Shed near Hmawza Ry. Station. Exhibit
18. Rangoon Museum Exhibits Nos. 1/6, 2/6, 3/6.
19. *Ibid*, Nos. 8/6, 9/6, 10/6.
20. An.-Rep. A. S. Burma, 1926, p. 35.
21. *Ibid.*, 1923, pp. 27-28.

2 Viṣṇu or Nārāyaṇa

Viṣṇu is the second but the most ancient and popular deity of the Hindu Triad. In India, South and North, he is worshipped in every house as a family deity, and at all auspicious occasions as well. Tradition has set forth that in his *Trivikrama* incarnation he placed one foot on the *Bhūloka* or the earth-world, another on the *Antarīkṣaloka* or the mid-world between heaven and earth, and a third on the *Pālālaloka* or the nether-world; the three worlds were thus entirely conquered. And what is recorded in tradition is, as it were, translated in actual history of the life and career of the god. One of the deities that was earliest to be elaborated in the Brahmanical pantheon, *Viṣṇu* early came to be recognised in Northern India as the most important god, and, then gradually in the South, as only next to *Śiva.* But his third stride was yet to be placed, and that beyond the seas in the Indian colonies of Java and Sumatra, Campa, and Kamboj, as well as in Siam, and, as we shall see, in Burma too, a country professedly Buddhist in religion. Thus, in Campa, *Viṣṇu* was known in various names such as *Nārāyaṇa, Hari, Govinda,* etc. Stories referring to his churning of the ocean, his raising of the world by his two hands, and the like are often-times mentioned in inscriptions; and, as in India, his different incarnations probably claimed greater homage than the god himself. In Kamboj, he was known as *Hari, Acyuta, Nārāyaṇa, Upendra, Vāsudeva, Keśava, Murārī,* etc.; his consort *Lakṣmī* or Śrī too was known and received her share of worship. Though he could not claim a very large following as did *Śiva,* he is, nevertheless, often mentioned in inscriptions and his images too were widely worshipped. In Siam, where Brahmanism preceded Buddhism, place names such as *Ban Phra Narai* (village of *Viṣṇu*) or *Khas Narai* (mountain of *Viṣṇu)* still point to a strong and early *Vaiṣṇava* tradition that had once been current in the Peninsula. But more exact are the finds of *Viṣṇu* images, *Viṣṇu* often on the back of *Garuḍa* or with *Lakṣmī.* Buddha is also often included as one of his ten *avatāras.* In Java he was still more popular. Her kings have aspired to attain the position of *Viṣṇu* himself and have not unoften identified themselves with him. Temples have been dedicated to him, in inscriptions honourable mention has been made of him, and one of his ten *avatāras—Rāma—*had been most popularly known. The Rāmāyaṇa as well as the *Kṛṣṇāyaṇa* have been translated in stone on the walls of *Prambanam* and *Panataram* temples. No less popular is *Viṣṇu* himself with his *Garuḍa.*

But little is known of his position in Burma. Stray finds of Vaiṣṇavite images in the Peninsula are things of common knowledge; but the history of his penetration thereto, the extent and character of his influence and the variety of his forms are but very poorly known. Prints of his third stride in Burma are yet to be traced.

The earliest *Vaiṣṇava* tradition in Burma is connected with Hmawza or old Prome, one of the oldest seat of kingship in Burma. The city is said to have been founded by a *Ṛṣi* whose name the Burmese Chronicles have failed to take into notice. *Mahayazawin,* the Burmese text that describes the foundation of the city states that the *Ṛṣi* who presided over the function was helped by six other divines—*Gavampati, Indra, Nāga, Garuḍa, Caṇḍī* and *Parameśvara.* Now *Gavampati, Indra* and *Nāga,* or a *Nāgarāja,* have often been incorporated in Burmese legendary history in connection with the foundation of cities or erection of temples, obviously without caving any actual historical significance. But the legend helps us undoubtedly to assume that a strong Indian element with all its traditions of town-planning and temple-building had been at work at the bottom of all such traditions and their actual translation in monuments. *Gavampati,* who is represented in *Mōn* records as the son of the Lord Buddha, has rightly been styled as the *"patron saint of the Mōns"* as well as the *"patron saint of Pagan,"* and is evidently a creation of the legendary imagination of the *Mōns. Indra* is the king of the *devas* who must invariably be present at all important functions. The *Nāga* mentioned in the *Mahayazwin* is certainly *Katakarmmanāgarāja* mentioned in *Mōn* records as having assisted in the foundation of the city of *Sisit* or *Śrīkṣetra* (old Prome). *Garuḍa* is the mythical bird who has the proud privilege of being the *vāhana* of *Viṣṇu. Caṇḍī* is *Kālī* or *Karālī* or the *Devī,* the wife of *Śiva* who is mentioned here in the *Mahayazawin* as *Parameśvara.* The *Mahayazawin* tradition is most probably an adaptation from early Talaing records, but in becoming so it has retained only the epithet—*Rṣi*—of the founder of the city, but has failed to mention the name of the *Rṣi.* That this. was *Viṣṇu* is evident from the early *Mōn* lithic records in most of which the story of the foundation of *Sisit or Śrīkṣetra* is given in more or less detail. Let us quote from the Great inscription of the *Shwezigōn Pagoda.*[2]

> "The Lord Buddha smiled and *Ānanda* asked the cause of this smile; and the Lord spoke unto *Ānanda—Ānanda,* hereafter a sage named *Bisnu,* great in supernatural power, great in glory, possessing the five transcendental faculties, together with my son *Gavampati,* and king *Indra* and *Bissukarmmadevaput (putra)* and *Katakarmmanāgarāja,* shall build a city called *Sisit (Śrīkṣetra)."* "

Then again—"After the sage *Biṣṇu* has built the city of *Sisit,* he shall depart from thence (and) in the city of *Arimaddanapura* (Pagan) he shall become king *Śrī Tribhuvanāditya dhammarāja,* etc."

It is thus evident that the *Ṛṣi* is *Viṣṇu* who is considered to have founded the city of old Prome. The *Mōn* records include one *Bissukarmmadevaput*—son of *Viśvakarmā,* the divine architect, as one who was destined to assist in the foundation of *Śrīkṣetra* (old Prome), but, excludes *Garuḍa, Caṇḍī* and *Parameśvara* mentioned in the *Mahāyazawin.*

An important corroboration of this tradition is found in the fact that old Prome or Hmawza was known in ancient times as *Bissunamyo*—an equivalent of *Viṣṇupura,* that is, the city of *Viṣṇu*--which undoubtedly points to some 'sort of Viṣṇuite influence having, been at work at this old royal city of Lower Burma.[3] Apart from this, important find have been made here at Hmawza of images that are distinctly Vianuite in character. But before we turn to these images and to other icons of*Viṣṇu* found at different localities of Burma, it is .interesting to see how and to what extent *Viṣṇu* has been able to penetrate into the tangle of traditional legendary history of Burma. For our purpose; we are here concerned with a king around whom has grown up a long series of more or less legendary accounts in Burmese traditional history.

Kyanzittha, son of Anawratha, is the second important king of Pagan, who, as seen through the veil of tradition, is a fantastic hero of fairy tales. But, 'in his own inscriptions, with their strong ecclesiastical flavouring he is presented as a grave and religious, but, quite human monarch, taking a deep interest in the spiritual and temporal welfare of his people and actively contibuting to that by his piety and good works.' In almost all the early *Mōn* records which, in most cases, relate to his reign and achievements, he is invariably styled as Śrī Tribhuvanāditya *dhammarāja,* a title distinctly Sanskritic in character. A long birth-legend forms the introduction and framework of most of these records; just referred to. The legend refers to successive re-births of king

Kyanzitthaa fact confessedly Buddhist in colour and spirit. Thus, the Great Inscription of the *Shwezigōn Pagoda*, Pagan,[4] states :

"It was once upon a time when the Lord Buddha was dwelling in the *Jetavanavihāra* that the Lord Buddha saw that which was to come (to pass) thereafter for the advancement of the Lord Buddha's religion (namely) the coming of king *Śrī Tribhuvanāditya dhammarāja* in the city of *Arimaddanapura,* when a thousand six hundred and thirty years should have elasped after the Lord Buddha's attaining *Parinirvāṇa.* And consequently the Lord smiled."

The Lord *Ānan* (*i.e.*, Ānanda) who was present, asked the reason of this smile. 'What reason (was there) that my Lord smiled thus?' (Buddha replied) '*Ānan,* hereafter a sage named *Bisnu* great in supernatural power, great in glory, possessing the five trans cendental faculties, together with my son *Gavampati* and king *Indra)* and *Bissukarmmadevaput* and *Katakarmmanāgarāja* shall build a city called *Sisit (Śrīkṣetra* or old Prome). After that, the "sage *Bisnu* departing from thence shall go up to *Brahmaloka* (and) departing from *Brahmaloka* shall come to be born in the city of *Arimaddanapura* (and) shall bear the name of king *Śrī Tribhuvanāditya dhammarāja* (and) shall uphold my religion." Thus did the Lord Buddha tell the reason of that smile to the Lord *Ānan* (or Ānanda).

"At that time Lord *Gavampati* hearing the explanation of the Lord Buddha, did obeisance to the Lord Buddha; and then in order to elucidate the Lord Buddha's statement, questioned (him) thus : My Lord, did my Lord truly say that thereafter a sage named *Bisnu* together with me shall build the city of *Sisit* ?'"

'Truly *Gavampati,* thus (it is). The sage *Bisnu* shall build (it) together with thee. Therefore, *Gavampati,* go then to king *In (dra)* and speak unto him thus : "O King of *devas* ! Receive with deference the saying of the Lord Buddha : (to wit that) the sage named *Bisnu* who is great in supernatural power (and) glory, together with me shall build the city of *Sisit*. At that time, in all the (good) works of the sage *Bisnu,* do go and bestir thyself." After the sage *Bisnu* has built the city of *Sisit,* he shall depart from thence (and) in the city of *Arimaddanapura,* he shall become king *Sri Tribhuvanāditya dhammarāja* (and) shall uphold the religion of the Buddha."[5]

But a different version of this birth-legend relating to *Srī Tribhuvanāditya dhammarāja* is given in the Myakan inscription of Myinpagan, Pagan, as also in two other inscriptions.[6] 'The Myakan inscription states :

"At the time when life (lasted) for twenty thousand years the Lord Buddha Kassapa came into existence in this world and found a resting place at the city of Benares and there dwelt in the *Isipatanamigadāvamahāvihāra.* At that time our Lord, this (present) king of the Law, was a wealthy man ...... Having lived to the term of his life (he) departed from thence (and) came into existence in a family of kings in the city of Patna ......(There) carrying out the ten duties of a king and after living to the term of his life, (he) departed from thence (and) came into existence in the family of King Rāma in the city of Oudh. (There- too) after having lived to the term of his life, (he) departed from thence; and in the time of the coming of our Lord the Buddha *Śākyamuni,* he was the sage *Bisnu* ...who dwelt upon a silver (mountain?) named *Kalasaparvata* ... "[7]

Here, the thread, of story, as recorded in the Great *Śwezigōn* inscription, is taken up, and the Myakan inscription goes on to relate what is more elaborately recorded in the *Shwezigōn* record, *i.e.,* the prophecy of Buddha to the effect that the sage *Bisnu* together with *Gavampati, Indra, Bissukarmmadevaput Katakarmmanāgarāja* shall build the city of *Sisit,* and then, from thence shall go into existence in *Brahmāloka,* and then again a thousand six hundred and thirty years after the Buddha's *parinirvāṇa* shall become king of the Law, in the city of *Arimaddanapura* and bear the name of *Śrī Tribhuvanacditya dhammarāja.*

We thus get the birth-legend in two versions. According to the first version which is shorter but more elaborate than the second, king *Śrī Tribhuvanāditya dharmmarāja* Kyanzittha is presented as having been in one of his earlier incarnations the sage *Viṣṇu* himself who lived contemporaneously with the Buddha. According to the second version, which prefaces the *Viṣṇu* episdde by three of the king's still earlier existences, the king is presented as having been a, wealthy and pious man living at Benares in Buddha Kassapa's time. In his next incarnation, he was born in the family of the kings of Patna, and in the third, in the royal house of the Rāma dynasty of Oudh. Next in the time of the Buddha *Śākyamuni,* he was a sage named *Viṣṇu.* There is an amount of difference in the two versions; but one thing is common to both, namely, that the king was in one of his previous births a sage named *Viṣṇu.* It is, therefore, obvious that he wanted to claim his identity with *Viṣṇu,* and this is certainly significant in view of the fact that Kyanzittha himself was a devout Buddhist initiated into the religion by his master Shin Arahan, and the records of his reign are frankly Buddhist inspirit and colour. Secondly, tradition, even then, was incessant in telling that *Sisit* or old Prome was built by *Viṣṇu* himself. Thirdly, *Viṣṇu* was considered not as a god but as a sage who was living contemporaneously with the Buddha himself, and it is evident from the fact noted above that the sage *Viṣṇu* held a position in Burma inferior to that of the Buddha, for, Kyanzittha dared not claim his identity with the great spiritual Lord of the creed he professed, but satisfied himself by identifying him as an incarnation of the sage *Viṣṇu*. In India, by the 11th and 12th centuries to which period our records belong, the Buddha had already come to be incorporated in the Brahmanical pantheon as one of the incarnations of *Viṣṇu*; and hence occupy a position subordinate to that of *Viṣṇu*. But there seems to have been an inverted process in Burma, for here *Viṣṇu* himself (and not the Buddha) did come to occupy a subordinate position: This was only natural, for Burma was professedly Buddhist all the time, while in India, Buddhism had come to be supplanted by neo-Brahmanism of the *Purāṇas*.

Viṣṇu as *Nārāyaṇa* seems also to have been known to the Hindu colonists of Burma. Even a casual reader of the early, *Mōn* records would be able to observe that *Brāhmaṇas* are often mentioned in them as taking part as priests in all religious ceremonies of the court. This is not at all to be surprised at, for, from Burma to Campa, as well as in Java, Sumatra and Bali; the *Brāhmaṇas* always played an active and influential part in the courts, no matter whether the religion was Brahmanism or Buddhism. These *Brāhmaṇas* in the Buddhist courts of Burma were evidently worshippers of *Viṣṇu*, mentioned in the inscriptions as Nārāyaṇa. The inscription found near the Tharaba gate, Pagan,[8] a record detailing an elaborate ceremonial attending the building of a fivefold pavilion *(Pañcaprāsāda)* in connection, as alleged, with king Kyanzittha's royal anointment, has numerous references to *Brāhmaṇas* who are constantly engaged in bringing water of lustration in vessels of gold, silver, brass and earthen ware and who are invariably mentioned as having worshipped *Nārāyaṇa* before they were required to perform any priestly duty. Thus :

> "(At) all these seventeen places they *(Brāhmaṇa* astrologers) made a decoration of plantains and adorned

with young plantains (and) sugarcane (and set ?) water (in) vessels of gold (and) silver (and) water (in) conch-shells wherein (they) put cleaned rice (and) *dubbā* grass, (and) spread mats, (with) golden flowers, altar oblations and altar candles. Having (arranged them?) *they made ink honour of Nārāyaṇa*, a decoration of plantains (called) "ox nose" adorned with young plantains (and) sugar cane (and) within it (set), boiled rice in cup-shaped vessels with candles stuck in it, (and) altar oblations, (and) they ... ... (brought?) water (in) vessels of gold (and) silver, spread mats (and) offered golden flower (and altar candles?). Then the *Brāhmaṇa astrologers worshipped Nārāyaṇa*. At the auspicious time : *godhūli* (being) *lagna*, the expert *Brāhmaṇa* astrologers bathed the side pillars, the *yas* pillars, etc."[9]

And again....." The expert *Brāhmaṇa* astrologers wore loin cloths, *sukhoy cindraw* (and) *sukhoy ular*, with *kucom* skirts of white. Then they went and worshipped *Nārāyaṇa*. (At) all the ten points they made decorations of plantains (and) altar oblations; water (in) vessels of gold and silver, (and) water in conch-shells wherein (they) put cleaned rice (and) *dubbā* grass, they arranged near by."[10]

This ceremonial is again and again detailed in the inscription and almost invariably in the same form. The worship of *Nārāyaṇa* seems thus to have been in vogue with its peculiarly Brahmanical ritual and it was not only tolerated by the Buddhist court and people, but, as it seems from the context of the inscription, was also considered as an indispensable item of all court ceremonies.

This mention of *Nārāyaṇa*-worship most probably refers to the worship of *Nārāyaṇa-śilā*.[11] It The context of the inscription as wept as repeated mention of the worship of the god seem to point to the fact that the god was almost in daily worship by the *Brāhmaṇas*. But nowhere is it given to understand that any image of the god was ever made and worshipped. Had it been so, it would have been possible for us to discover more images of the god than have hitherto been found at Pagan where the inscription has been discovered and of which place the record gives us the story. The only vestiges of *Viṣṇu* worship in Pagan are the remains of a temple known locally as *Nat-hlaung kyaung,* in which there were once housed images of the ten *avatāras* of *Viṣṇu* and of the god himself. Stray finds have also been made of bronze *Viṣṇu* images, but the mention of *Nārāyaṇa* in the above record does not seem to point to these bronze or stone images, or to any *Viṣṇu* temple. It is a matter of common knowledge that the *Nārāyaṇa-śilā* was and still is the most important object of daily worship in every orthodox *Brāhmaṇa* house in Northern and Southern India; and it is probable that the god was likewise worshipped by the emigrant *Brāhmaṇas* also, especially on the eve of their performing any priestly duty.

Images

We have already noticed the association of a strong Viṣṇuite tradition with Hmawza or old Prome. Here have been unearthed several Viṣṇuite images that are most probably the oldest in Burma. We have here to consider three important slabs[12]—all housed at present in the *Phongyi kyaung* museum near the Hmawza Railway Station—representing three different types of the god.

The first (fig. 2) is a rectangular slab of soft sand-stone carved out in comparatively bold relief representing two figures standing side by side but apart from one another. The figure in the right is one of *Viṣṇu* standing on a Garuḍa with its tail and wings outstretched, a fact very ably represented on the slab with a touch of abstract naturalism. The head and portions of the neck of the human bust of the bird have been lost, but what remains is sufficient to guarantee that the animal represented is nothing but a *Garuḍa,* the celebrated carrier of *Viṣṇu.* To the left of *Viṣṇu* on a full-blown double-petalled lotus, represented no doubt in a somewhat abstract manner, stands *Lakṣmī,* the consort of *Viṣṇu.* It is most unfortunate that the upper portion of the slab has been damaged to such an extent that both the figure have lost their heads, and *Viṣṇu* his upper right hand in addition. Otherwise the figures are very well-preserved and even the details can easily be read. The god has four hands, the attribute in the upper right is lost the lower right which is raised up to the chest holds a round object, evidently a *vilva* or *mātuliṅga* fruit; the upper left, so far as discernible on the stone, holds the *cakra* (wheel), and the lower left the *gadā* (mace)—unlike, indeed, the type generally held by the god. The goddess has two hands, the right one which is raised up to the shoulders holds, as it seems, a bunch of lotus stems, and the left hangs lightly downwards. The sculpture from iconographic point of view is important in more than one respect. First, the holding of a *vilva* or *mātuliṅga* fruit—an attribute of *Śiva* and *Lakṣmī*—by *Viṣṇu* is undoubtedly quite unique; it is never the custom in India; in the colonies we have yet scarcely any similar instance, nor have we any such reference in any known version of texts on *Pratimā-lakṣaṇam.* If it is a *vilva,* it is likely that the attribute associated with *Lakṣmī* has here come to be transposed to become an attribute of *Lakṣmī's* Lord *Viṣṇu.* Secondly, the position of the *gadā* or the mace held in the left lower hand is also somewhat peculiar; it is generally held in the hand with all the five fingers with its stout bottom directed upwards and tapering top downwards; in other instances, the hand is placed on the top of the *gadā* which rests on the floor.[13] But here it is held at the neck with its stout bottom hanging downwards but not resting on the ground. But apart from these attributes the sculpture has other interesting iconographic features.

Neither in India nor in the colonies we have knowledge of any such image as the present one where *Viṣṇu* and *Lakṣmī* stand side by side. Images of *Krṣṇa* and *Rukmiṇī* or of *Lakṣmī* with *Viṣṇu* in his *Narasiṁha* or *Varāha* incarnation[14] are frequently seen, but *Viṣṇu* with his consort *Lakṣmī* standing side by side on their respective *vāhanas* is indeed very rare; we scarcely know of any such example.[15] We have no doubt references to *Lakṣmī-Nārāyaṇa* images in *Pratimā-lakṣaṇam* text; *e.g.*, in the *Viśvakarma- Śāstram* we have:—

Lakṣmī-Nārāyaṇau kāryyau saṁyuktau divarūpiṇau
Dakṣiṇasthā vibhor-mūrtir-lakṣmī-mūrtis-to vāmataḥ/
Dakṣiṇaḥ kaṇṭhalagno'syā vāmo hastas-sarojabhṛt
Vibhor-vāmakaro lakṣmyāḥ kukṣibhāga-sthitaḥ sadā//

In the *Rūpamaṇḍanam*, we read :—

"Ubhau ca dvibhujau kuryyāl-lakṣmīṁ Nārāyaṇā-śritam
Daivaṁ śastraiḥ svakiyaiśca Garuḍopari saṁsthitam/
Dakṣiṇaḥ kaṇṭhalagno'syā vāmo hastas-sarojadhṛk
Vibhor-vāmakaro lakṣmyāḥ kukṣibhāgaḥ-sthitaḥ sadā//

Thus, according to the *Viśvakarma-Śāstram, Viṣṇu* should be represented to the right *of Lakṣmī* whose left hand should hold a lotus and the right wind round the neck of her consort; whereas the left hand of the god himself should stretch to the left armpit of *Lakṣmī*. The attribute or function of the right hand of the god is not mentioned; but it is necessary to present the *vāhana* as well as the two other attributes *śaṅkha* and *cakra* as two *āyudhapuruṣas (kartavyaṁ vāhanaṁ devādhobhāgagaṁ sadā;* and, *śaṅkha-cakradharau tasya dvau kāryyau puruṣau puraḥ).* The *Rūpamaṇḍanam* explicitly says that the deities should have only two hands each, that *Viṣṇu* should stand upon his *vāhana Garuḍa,* that *Lakṣmī* should embrace his lord by winding her right hand round his neck and hold in her left a lotus, and that *Viṣṇu* should stretch his left hand up to the armpit of his consort. The two versions are almost similar, but it is interesting to see how the present icon deviates from all known texts. The god, instead of having two, has four hands and the goddess, who was two hands only, does hold the lotus in her right, not in the left. She does not wind her right hand round the neck of *Viṣṇu*, nor does *Viṣṇu* stretch his left to her armpit. This is not all. A further point of departure from Indian icons is the fact that the god and the goddess, both standing, have been given equal importance, their height is almost the same, and though they do not stand on the same plane, it is easily seen that the goddess has not been subordinated to the god which is generally the practice in India. The one factor alone which attaches greater importance to the god is his four hands, while *Lakṣmī* has got only two. These deviations can only be accounted for when it is said that the Indian colonists of the Peninsula had either followed a different textual version yet unknown; or, colonists as they were, they had been less bound down by textual canons than their less fortunate brethren at home. That was why they could easily evolve new forms and types out of their imagination unhampered by any tradition.

The second important piece of icon from Hmawza is also one of *Viṣṇu,* standing on his *Garuḍa* and represented on a stone slab having the form of an isosceles triangle.[15] The stone is about sixteen inches high and about a foot wide at the base. The material is a poor kind of very soft porous sand-stone, and the workmanship is rough and clumsy. It is the product of an entirely local school of art which finds expression not only in the typical cut of the face and the simple, almost foolish, smile on the two lips, but most remarkably in. the dress the god wears. He stands on his *Vāhana Garuḍa* with two heavy outstretched wings, the left of which alone remains; it is, therefore, difficult to decide whether the bird was represented with a human fact and bust as in the medieval sculptures of Eastern and Southern

India, or with those more realistic features of a bird as in Indian colonial art. But what remains on the stone, seems to favour the former assumption, namely, that the bird represented is really an animal with a human bust and a bird-like lower portion almost exactly as in Indian art. In the present case the wings of the bird have not been so elaborately and so realistically portrayed as in the one discussed above; rather they are done in a more abstract manner and are meant as if to represent the leafy branches of a tree; yet there is sufficient to show that the artist knew his subject well but failed to give an artistic expression to it. The god has four hands; the two upper raised upwards hold the *cakra* and *śaṅkha* and the two lower hold again a *vilva* or *mātuliṅga* fruit and the *godā* respectively. He is elaborately decorated with ornaments having wristlets, armlets and a richly carved *keyūra* round his neck; the head-dress which must have been an elaborate one is, unfortunately enough, broken, but, it is most likely that it was of the kind so often seen in Burmese sculptures where it is invariably associated with all important personages and divinities. We are accustomed to see in India and in the colonies *Viṣṇu* as riding or seated crossed-legged on his *vāhana; Viṣṇu,* standing on *Garuḍa* is rare; in fact, such representations are hardly seen. It is most interesting that the type has up till now been found in Burma alone, and that in more than one example. In Java the famous *Airlaṅga-Viṣṇu* statue[17] is, in fact, represented as seated, though it gives the impression of an erect figure. But it may be recognised, it seems, that in the colonies, there is a general tendency to represent the gods as standing, rather than as seated, on their *vāhanas,* specially when their *vāhanas,* are birds. A parallel instance in point is the famous *Skanda* or *Kārtikeya* image[18] of Mysōn in Campa standing erect on his *vāhana* the peacock. This gives us, it seems, a glimpse into the imagination of the colonial artists—an imagination that seems to have liked to unravel itself in comparatively more effective dramatic poses and situations and, therefore, less traditional and conventional, though the execution was not always up to it. The *Airlaṅga-Viṣṇu* statue, just referred to, though really seated, gives, in fact, the impression, as we have said, of an erect figure and the pose of the god, more so of the *Garuḍa,* is most dramatic.

We now turn to the third important Viṣṇuite sculpture (15½"X14½") from Hmawza.* Apparently it is a plastic representation of the well-known mythology of *Śeṣa* or *Ananta-śayāna Viṣṇu* (fig. 4). It is the most important of the reclining forms of *Viṣṇu* who is here supposed to sleep on the coils of the serpent *Ananta* that shields the head of the god of gods under its five or seven hoods. By the side of the serpent couch near the feet of *Viṣṇu* is often represented the kneeling figure of *Lakṣmī* in a worshipping attitude (*cf.* Plate XXXI, G. Rao's Hindu Iconography, Vol. I, Part 1), or the seated figure of *Bhūmidevī* or *Lakṣmī* (*cf.* Plate XXXII, G. Rao, *ibid.,)* who holds the right foot of the god in her hands. He is said to have two or four hands and from his navel springs a lotus stalk with a full blossomed lotus flower on which *Brahmā* is comfortably seated. *Brahmā, Śiva* and *Indra* are also sometimes represented as subsidiary deities; and *Jaya* and *Vijaya* as two attendants. The attributes of the god are represented in their own form or as personified.

In the present example from Hmawza, the god is represented as lying straight with his two legs crossed at the

---

* This, and the image just described were discovered at a village named Kalagangōn near Hmawza. Here have recently been discovered "a few fragments of a Hindu sculpture or of perhaps several such sculptures .... but, unfortunately, most of them are too small to admit of any identification." (An. Rep., A.S. India, 1926-27, p. 182.) Near this village there was a mound called Khin-bha-gōn in the course of excavation of which was discovered a hand carved in standstone, and holding a conch which had probably belonged to an image of *Viṣṇu.* (*Ibid.*, pp. 171 ff),

ankles. The head with the usual head-dress rests on a higher plane and the body stretches not on the coils of a serpent but, so far as it seems, on a lotus couch that rests on a *makara* the head of which is clearly visible on the left corner at the bottom of the slab. This is peculiarly interesting, for we have not yet been able to discover any sculpture or text where the reclining *Viṣṇu* is ever represented as having any association with *makara*. The usual practice, as we have already seen, is to represent him as reclining directly on the serpent *Ananta*. It is, therefore, striking, and can only be accounted for by assuming that the colonial artists either followed a text which is yet unknown to us or that they; misinterpreted the whole story as known in India. This will be more evident from the fact that from *Viṣṇu's* navel rises not one single lotus-stalk but three such stalks with, three fullblown lotuses on which are seated the three gods of the Hindu Trinity—*Viṣṇu*, the main deity, with his four hands holding the different attributes (the right lower which is raised up to the chest holds again a *vilva* or *mātuliṅga* fruit), is seated at the centre; he is flanked by *Brahmā* to the right and *Śiva* to the left. The latter, as usual in India, is generally seated by the side of *Viṣṇu* as in an example, from Mahavalipuram, or as mounting his bull *Nandī* in the air as in another from Deogarh. *Brahmā* is here, as elsewhere, seated cross-legged on the lotus rising from the navel of *Viṣṇu*, He has four hands, the two lower joined in the *añjali* pose, and is endowed, as usual, with four heads—three of which are actually represented—crowned over with his peculiar *jaṭā-mukuṭa*. All these three figures, separately haloed by lotus petal designs, are meant to hold equal status, subordinate only to the main deity—*Viṣṇu*, who is here represented as reclining. The figures are dressed up to the knees and have usual ornaments in the ears, arms, ankles, neck and waist. The position of the right legs of the seated figures of *Viṣṇu* and Śiva as well as that of the two legs of the reclining figure are interesting. In the former-case, it is raised upwards, while in, the latter they are crossed. An almost similar position of the two legs of reclining *Viṣṇu*, may be seen in the *Yogaśayānāmūrti* relief from Aihole, illustrated on Plate XXXIII of Rao's Hindu Iconography, Vol. I, Part I.

Two similar sculptures (figs. 5 and 6) from the iconogrąphic point of view are known from Thātoñ[19] or ancient Rammaññadesa, the land *par excellence* of the Talaings. Unlike the two sculptures from Hmawza just discussed above, these are carved out in bold and round relief on comparatively hard reddish sandstone and are frankly works, not of local Burman craftsmen, but of Indian colonial artists. Their general features and ornaments as well as the form and spirit that find expression in them are undoubtedly Indian. The aristic and historical interest of these sculptures, which we shall discuss later on, are far more than one can possibly, imagine. They are by far the most interesting specimens which bring out in more prominent relief the relation of a particular school of the colonial art of Burma with a contemporary Indian school of art on this side of the Bay of Bengal. But here we must content ourselves with a study of them from the iconographic point of view alone.

The two slabs measure 3½'×1'10" and 4½'×3' respectively. The smaller one (fig. 5) which is a rectangular slab rounded off at the top represents at the bottom the reposing or *a Śyānamūrti* of *Viṣṇu.* His legs are crossed as in the example from Hmawza but in a more easy and flexible manner, and his four hands hold their respective attributes—the two upper which lie flat and reach up to the shoulder seem to hold the *cakra* (discus) and *śaṅkha* (conch-shell) respectively, while the lower right placed upon the lower chest holds a round object, most probably a *vilva* or *mātuliṅga* fruit; the lower left, placed alongside the thigh, holds something that is difficult to be recognised. His clothes reach up to the knee and he wears ornaments that are frankly Indian—round the wrists, ankles, waist and neck. The head-dress which consists of triangular lobes pointing upwards had already come to be well familiarised in the medieval sculptures of the Eastern School. The three lotus stalks supposed to have sprung from the navel of the god are actually carved out on the stela itself and are represented as having risen from the back of the lying figure. Upon the petals of the three lotus stalks are seated in *padmāsana* three divinities, *Brahmā, Viṣṇu,* and *Śiva;* at the top of them are represented three stele, the middle one being more prominent than the other two, signifying obviously the more prominent position of *Viṣṇu* who is seated just below. *Brahmā* seated to the right is represented with three heads with his usual head-dress, ornaments and clothes that reach up almost to the anklet. His right hand is raised up to the chest and the left rests upon his left knee. Śiva seated to the left holds in his right hand raised up to the chest probably the *mātuliṅga* fruit and in his left raised up to the shoulder the *triśūla* or the trident. *Viṣṇu* who is seated in the middle holds in his upper right the *cakra* and in the corresponding left the *śaṅkha.* The right lower seems to have been represented in the *jñāna-mudrā* pose and the lower left is unfortunately mutilated. The description thus detailed would at once warrant us to conclude that it is a representation of the well-known *Anantaśayyā* episode of *Viṣṇu.* But we are for once put into doubt for missing the coils of the serpent *Ananta* on which he is supposed to lie; there is not even any suggestion of them. The whole slab is in a fair state of preservation, and the figures are all carved in bold and round relief, the details are all elaborately shown, and had the coils of the serpent been actually represented, we have no reason to miss them. It seems that the artist probably satisfied himself by scratching down on the slab, the outlines alone of the five heads of the serpent which are seen at the top of the head-dress as an ornamental aureole.

Almost exactly of the same iconographic peculiarities is the larger slab from Thātoñ (fig. 6). It represents the same episode, the *Anantasayyā* scene of *Viṣṇu* who, here too, is seen lying in a reposing attitude with his legs crossed and his upper two hands holding the *śaṅkha* and the *padma* respectively. The whole slab is badly damaged and the details are difficult to be made out. Yet the coils of the serpent seem here to have been represented, and the five hoods above the head-dress are more prominently shown. There is also an attempt at realism in the representation of water which is suggested by crowded lotus leaves, lotus stems and buds in the midst of which the god rests on the serpent. The same sense of realism is also noticeable in the fact that the main lotus stalk is here shown to have really sprung from the navel. It winds upwards to a point where it becomes three different stalks with three full-blown lotuses on which are again seated *Brahmā, Viṣṇu,* and *Śiva* with three stele at their back. *Viṣṇu,* in the middle is seated cross-legged, but the two other divinities have their right legs raised upwards with the palm resting on the ground. It should be noticed that the stela at the back of *Viṣṇu,* though much broken off, is higher and more prominent than those of *Brahmā* and *Śiva,* signifying no doubt the superior position of *Viṣṇu* in the Brahmanical Trinity.

There are two other figures of *Viṣṇu* in the Rangoon Museum. One is a small (about 10 × 4 inches) standing figure of the god with four hands and with a halo round the head which is crowned with a peculiar head-dress. The lower left hand holds the *gadā* and the right, slightly bent, touches the waist. Two more hands did exist, of them the upper left seems to have held a pointed lotus bud. The material is soft reddish sandstone, and the sculpture is worked out in bold relief. It probably formed part of a temple as a decorative figure and stylistically seems to belong to the 9th century A.D. The material as well as the style and workmanship of the sculpture seem to relate it with the two Thātoñ sculptures described above.

The second, a standing figure of *Viṣṇu,* belonging to at least four centuries later than the one just discussed, *i.e.*, to about the 14th century A.D., was discovered at Mergui but has lately been brought over to the Rangoon Museum. The material is a piece of rough porous sand-stone greyish in colour, and the crude and rough workmanship is late South Indian in character. The piece is little less than two feet in height, and though the figure stands with a stele at the back, it is carved out in comparatively bold relief though the execution is certainly poor it represents a standing Hindu deity with four hands heavily laden with ornaments and crowned over with a peculiar *kirīṭa-mukuṭa.* The two legs are covered with anklets almost up to the knee joint, and on the two sides of the conical head-dress seem to have stretched two locks of matted hair. The two upper hands seem to have held the *śaṅkha* and *cakra* respectively; the lower right hand seems to be in the *abhayamudrā* or protection-affording pose, while the lower left is in the *varada* or boon-conferring pose. It is one of the most common *sthānaka-mūrtis* of *Viṣṇu;* but whether it is a *yogasthānaka* or *bhogasthānaka-mūrti* it is difficult to decide. In the *sthānaka-mūrtis* of these two classes the left lower hand is generally made to rest on the left hip, whereas, the same hand in the present example is represented in the *varada* pose; but in other details the icon closely follows the South Indian canon.

The Nāt-hlaung Temple and its Gods

Earlier than this, but later in date than the images from Hmawza or from Thātoñ described above, is the group of Viṣṇuite sculptures discovered in and belonging to the

Nāthlaung kyaung at Pagan, the only ancient *Viṣṇu* temple now extant in Burma (fig. 1). It is an interesting monument, not so much from the viewpoint of architecture, as it is from the viewpoint of history and the cult it represents. "The name," says Mon. Duroiselle, "implies that it was built for housing not figures of the Buddha, but statues of deities inferior to him; in this case Hindu figures." "In fact, it is a *Viṣṇu* temple enshrining in the niches of its walls as well as in those of the central obelisk, figures of the different incarnations of *Viṣṇu* and having as its principal deity one image of *Viṣṇu* seated on his *vāhana Garuḍa* placed in the main sanctum, formed by a large deep niche in the middle of the east face of the central obelisk. According to tradition it was founded by King Taung Thugyi who lived from *c.* 931-964 A.D., a date too early for the style of the building itself as well as for the style of the sculptures decorating its walls; nor is there any epigraphic or literary evidence to support so early a date. "The only mention in Burmese of a Hindu temple built at Pagan, is found in a late manuscript called *Pugan Mro Phura Samon,* or Record of the Pagan Pagodas, where it is said that it was built by King Anaorahta after his return from the conquest of Thātoñ (1057 A.D.). This might well be the case, but in the absence of any authoritative corroboration, and in the light of the fact borne out by epigraphs—that Anaorahta was then a very fervent adherent of the Simhalese form of Southern Buddhism, it is doubtful whether this bigoted prince would have gone to the length of building a Hindu temple." Curiously enough, as Mon. Duroiselle has already pointed out, there has been discovered an inscription recording the erection of a *Viṣṇu,* temple at Pagan. The epigraph purports to say a *Vaiṣṇava* saint named *Irayiran Siriyan,* a resident of *Magodayarpattanam* in *Mali Maṇḍalam* and a disciple of *Śrī Kulaśekhara* "made a *maṇḍapa,* gave a door" in the temple of "*Nānādeśī Vinnagara Alavar* at *Pukam,* alias *Arivattanapuram. Magodayarpattanam* in *Mali*

Maṇḍalam is Cranganore in Malabar; *Pukam* is certainly *Pugāmā* of the *Kalyāṇī* inscriptions and *Pukhan* or *Pugan* of Chinese travellers; and *Arivattanapura* is obviously *Arimaddanapura,* another name of the royal city of Pagan. "*Nānādeśī Vinnagara* means," says Hultzsch, "the *Viṣṇu,* temple of those coming from various countries. This name shows that the temple which was situated in the heart of the Buddhist country of Burma had been founded and was resorted to by *Vaiṣṇavas* from various parts of the Indian Peninsula."[21] As *Nāt-hlaung kyaung* is the only *Vaiṣṇava* temple that is still extant at Pagan, and as there is no reference to any other *Vaiṣṇava* monument of this place in literature or inscriptions, it is natural to infer, as Mon. Duroiselle has done, that the *Nāt-hlaung kyaung* is the very temple referred to in the Tamil inscription. But from the record itself, it is clear that the temple had already existed there when the *maṇḍapa* was made and the "door was given to it." Hultzsch refers the inscription to the 13th century A.D. on paleographic grounds, and as the inscription records the gift of the *maṇḍapa* and the door—not the erection of the temple itself—it is a likely assumption that the temple had been built before the 13th century. It is, therefore, quite likely that the tradition contained in the Burmese manuscript referred to above is true; and that Anawrahta, who flourished in the last half of the 11th century A.D., could have well built the temple—a date which can in no way be deemed early for the architectural or sculptural style of the temple or of the gods respectively. Anawrahta was indeed a fervent adherent of the Simhalese form of Southern Buddhism; but when we read through the contemporary *Mōn* records, and remember that in the Pagan Court the *Brāhmaṇas* played a very prominent part not only in rituals and ceremonies of the court but also as court-astrologers, and that these *Brāhmaṇas* who were worshippers of *Nārāyaṇa Viṣṇu,* required a place, of worship for their own community, we can easily appreciate that Anawrahta himself allowed this prerogative to the most honoured *Brāhmaṇa* priests of his court who, it may be surmised, had approached him with their request and whom the king wanted not to displease.

From the traces on the outer walls of the eastern or the entrance face of the shrine, as well as from the raised yard in front of the temple itself, it seems that there was originally a porch or a vestibule which was probably identical, with the *maṇḍapa* referred to in the Tamil inscription just discussed. But, unfortunately, this porch or *maṇḍapa* which did not form part of the original structure has crumbled down to pieces, and the foundation only remains. The doorway has a store frame of which the lintel has broken down; and, if our surmise can still be pushed, it is this stone-frame door that is referred to in the inscription ('door was given to it'), as having been made a gift of by the *Vaiṣṇava* saint. The broken lintel has now been replaced by a beam of re-inforced concrete.

In plan, the *Nāt-hlaung kyaung* is a square raised on a pannelled and moulded plinth about five feet high above the ground. Like a good number of other temples in Pagan, the interior of the square is occupied by the usual perambulatory corridor running all round a huge central square masonry structure on three faces of which there were originally figures of gods standing in niches adorned with pilasters. On the outer walls of the square basement there are, as we have already noticed, a number of arched niches each of which originally contained one stone sculpture. Most of them are nor lost; one or two have been carried over to other countries; and a few that still remain *in situ* are more or less badly damaged. In the niches of the interior square obelisk there were originally standing images of *Viṣṇu* of which one is comparatively well-preserved. Of the ten outer sculptures that represent the ten *avatāras* of *Viṣṇu*, seven only remain; "three of the four niches on the east side are empty, the sculptures having apparently been removed from them and destroyed by icono clasts; the figures that remain bear visible traces of wilful disfiguration."

Let us begin by describing the main deity of the temple. It has already been noticed that the centre of the interior is occupied by a square obelisk. In the middle of the east face of this obelisk is a large deep niche where the principal figure was once enshrined. The identity of this principal figure was long unknown, and up till the first decade of this century the image itself was even known as lost. Colonel Yule, while visiting Pagan in the last quarter of the century, saw lying on the floor of this temple two images,[22] one standing and another seated, both of stone. The standing one is an image of *Śiva* now housed in the Ānanda Museum, Pagan;[23] while the seated one (4 ft. high) is an image of *Viṣṇu* on his *Garuḍa,* and has now found its place in the Berlin Museum.[24] The credit is due to Mon. Duroiselle who for the first time asserted that the principal figure of the temple should be identified with the god now housed in the Berlin Museum,[25] and pointed out that Col. Yule was wrong in describing this figure as coming from the niche above the capital on the left sanctum proper. The slab represents the figure of *Viṣṇu* seated on a lotus throne resting on *Garuḍa* (fig. 7). The whole piece of sculpture is executed in bold relief; the lotus petals of the seat are shown in sharp beautiful curves, the god is seated in *padmāsana* in a smiling repose, the carrier-bird *Garuḍa* poses itself as if it were about to fly and both the god and his *vāhana* are elaborately ornamented. from head downwards to the ankles. Beautiful *kirīṭa-mukuṭa* flanked by fluttering scarves on two side's crown the head of the god; ornaments round the arms, wrists and ankles are simple, but those at the ears, neck and the waist are profusely and elaborately executed. The presentation of the *Garuḍa* is peculiar and differs considerably from the two examples from Hmawza discussed above. The bird shows a short stunted human bust resting on two heavy rounded feet with a pair of heavy wings scratched in short rounded lines. The god holds in his upper hands the disc and the conch respectively. The palm of the lower right hand which is raised almost to the chest is, unfortunately, mutilated, so much so that the attribute can hardly be made out, but the position of the hand seems to indicate that it was probably a *vilva* or *mātuliṅga* fruit as is usually the case in Burma; the lower left holds the club, not at the top but round the middle. It is interesting to find in this example *Viṣṇu* seated on his *Garuḍa* as in Indian examples; and the pose and attitude too of the god and his carrier are more or less akin to similar sculptures from India. Interesting is also the lotus-seat that intervenes between *Viṣṇu* and *Garuḍa;* it seems that the bird and its flying attitude have practically lost their real artistic and iconographic significance and serve merely as decorations.

Over the two capitals on the two sides of the principal figure are two small niches (2 ft. high) that must have once housed two stone sculptures. Of these two, one still remains *in situ* (fig. 13). It is a small slab representing likewise the figure of *Viṣṇu* seated cross-legged *(padmāsana)* on a lotus-throne resting on a *Garuḍa* with outstretched wings. The figure is very badly mutilated, but enough remains to show beyond doubt that it is a *Garuḍa*. The god is ornamented with simple but heavy ornaments round the wrists and arms, but they are not so elaborate as in the example just noticed nor is there any *mukuṭa* of any description whatsoever. The head-dress is most simple and is similar to those so common on the heads of the innumerable Buddha figures of Burma of a later period; the dress is plain and 'resembles (Mon. Duroiselle points out) that of a Buddhist monk.' The iconography of the figure seems all the more interesting when we examine the attitude of the divinity and the physiognomy of the face which is peculiarly Burmese in character. Noticeable are also the two distended earlobes which is a distinctive feature of the Buddha icon. Rightly has it been, therefore, identified as the *Buddha avatāra* of *Viṣṇu*. The *vāhana Garuḍa*, and the attributes, such as the disc held in the second right hand on a level with the shoulder and the club held in the left arm resting on the knee, determine once for all the cult which the god belongs to.

On the northern, western and southern faces of the central obelisk, referred to above, were originally figures of three standing deities cut out in comparatively bold relief in brick within a niche flanked with slender pilasters. The figures are all very badly defaced, and the attributes can hardly be traced without difficulty. The three figures are replicas of one another; they are all of the same pose and attitude with graceful limbs beautifully adorned with ornaments richly carved. The position of the four hands are the same in each and it is most likely that they carried similar attributes too. One of the three is comparatively better preserved (fig. 8) and this is described by Mon. Duroiselle as follows : "the lower right arm is missing. The upper right hand holds what remains of a broken object, probably the disc. The lower left arm rests on the club traces of which are visible ....; the upper left hand holds the conch, the outlines of which are still perfectly seen ...... This last attribute shows it to be *Viṣṇu*. Similar traces of the once existing symbols are visible, but much more faintly, on the bricks behind two other statues."[28] The standing position which is most common to medieval *Viṣṇu* images of India, the smooth, refined and elegant modelling of the slender and well-proportioned body, the beautifully executed ornaments, and, above all, the physiognomy of the figures suffice to show that they are frankly Indian in character, belonging to a period not later than the 11th century A.D)., and stylistically have very close affinity with the contemporary medieval sculptural art of Eastern India.

We turn now to the images in the niches on the outer walls of the temple. The niche at the eastern end of the south wall is occupied by a representation of the *Varāha avatāra* of *Viṣṇu* (fig. 9). The figure is badly mutilated; the boar head and the *Bhūdevī* have suffered most, but the attitude of the legs and the position of the head turned towards the left shoulder on which the defaced female figure of the seated *Bhūdevī* can easily be noticed, hardly leave any doubt as to its identification. The heavy chignon of the goddess falling do her back and the hands clasped in adoration are represented with a creditable thoroughness of iconographic detail. The hands have mostly broken off; the attributes cannot, therefore, be recognised; but the mace *(gadā)* held at the middle by the left lower hand as well as the petals of the lotus throne are clearly distinguishable. It may be mentioned here that the attitude of the two legs which is generally determined by the attitude of the head has here been to some extent misunderstood. When the head is turned towards the left, it is natural for us, to expect from similar Indian examples as well as from artistic requirement that the left leg should be bent and the right kept straight and in order, or *vice versa*. But here in the present example, though the head is turned towards the left, the leg bent is the right one, not the left.

One of the niches is occupied by a representation of the *Nṛsiṁha* or *Narasiṁha avatāra* of *Viṣṇu* (fig. 10). The attitude of the legs with their knee-joints bent forward as well as the lower hands holding something on the lap is interesting, and is the determining factor for the identification of the divinity. The figure on the lap is completely gone, traces of the stone are only left, but the lines of the lion face of the principal figure with at least six hands that are visible, and the sharp nails of one of the hands that are used to tear off the body of *Hiraṇyakaśipu* that can yet be traced, leave no doubt as to its being the *Narasiṁha avatāra* of *Viṣṇu.*

The third niche is occupied by a sculpture representing a two-handed divinity standing erect on a lotus throne with the head slightly bent towards the left (fig. 11) It is crowned with the usually lobed head-dress flanked by fluttering scarves on two sides, but the face is mutilated and hardly can anything be made out. The god is dressed up to the knees and the hands holding respectively the arrow and the bow at once show that it is an image of *Rāmacandra avatāra* of *Viṣṇu*. Iconographic texts would lay down that "*Rāmacandra* should never have more than two arms; in the right hand the *bāṇa* or arrow should be held, and in the left hand the *dhanus* or the bow,"[27] and the present example strictly follows the text. But some of the texts demand that an image of *Śrī Rāma* should be a standing one '*with three bends in the body,* in other words, it has to be a standing image of the *tribhaṅga* variety,"[28] an injunction followed in most of the South Indian images of *Rāmāvatāra*. But here the injunction seems to have been disregarded; nor is the divinity accompanied by *Śītā, Lakṣmaṇa* or *Hanumān* as laid down in certain other, especially South Indian, texts.

The fourth niche of the temple is occupied by an image easily distinguishable as *Paraśurāma,* another *avatāra* of *Viṣṇu* (fig. 12). The figure stands on a lotus throne flanked by two fullblown lotuses; it is crowned by the usual head-dress and have also usual ornamental decorations. The attitude of the body is erect but the head is slightly bent towards the right. The hands, two in number, hold respectively a staff-like object perhaps a *khaḍga* or sword raised upwards, and an axe, resting on the left shoulder. The latter attribute determines the iconography of the sculpture. Here the icon differs a bit from written texts which lay down that

Paraśurāma should have the '*paraśu* or axe in the right hand, and the left hand should be in the *sūchi* pose as if pointing to something.'[29] But the *Agnipurāṇa* would have four hands for *Paraśurāmāvatāra* holding respectively the *paraśu, khaḍga, bāṇa,* and *dhanus;* this helps us to determine that the object held in the right hand of the divinity cannot be anything else than a *khaḍga* or sword.

Of the ten niches, we already know that three on the east side are empty, the icons have not yet been traced and there is very little hope of their recovery. Of the seven icons that remain, four namely, *Varāha, Narasiṁha, Rāmacandra* and *Paraśurāma* have already been identified without any very great difficulty. Of the rest, two are so badly defaced that it is difficult to be certain about their identification; in fact, no attempt has yet been made. The third is, however, one of the best-preserved images of the *Nāt-hlaung kyaung.* Mon. Duroiselle sought to identify it, but could not come to a decision. We begin then with this very image whose presence in a *Viṣṇu* temple is unique and interesting.

It would surprise all at the first instance to know that it is not an image of *Viṣṇu,* nor of any of his *avatāras.* It is sheltered in the niche to the proper left of the entrance (fig. 14) to the temple. The image can easily be described; but it is better to quote Mon. Duroiselle. "It is standing on a lotus flower from which two other smaller ones spring; the arms are placed close to the body bent upward at the elbows, and each hand holds a lotus bud on a level with the shoulders; it wears a crown; the distended earlobes hang down and touch the shoulder under the weight of large ear ornaments. It has bracelets, armlets and anklets; the lower garment is tucked up and reaches as far as the knees; lines showing the folds are vissible." Mon. Duroiselle was not able, as we have said, to identify it, but he added, "The number of niches would lead one to suppose that this also represents one of *Viṣṇu's avatāras;* but it has none of the distinctive attributes of any of these."[30] And, precisely for this reason, it is *not* one of the *avatāras* of *Viṣṇu,* but seems in all likelihood to be an image of *Sūrya* of the South Indian type. The position of the two hands as well as the lotus buds held in one line with the shoulders are significant; no less significant is the number of the hands, namely two, which is a distinctive feature of South Indian *Sūrya* images, and the strictly erect position of standing as well. The high boots covering the two feet and the horses drawing the chariot are, no doubt, missing in the present example; but it need not surprise us in the least, for *Sūrya* in South India does not generally wear boots nor rides a horse-drawn chariot. The iconographic affinity is, therefore, such that it is only natural for us to identify the present icon as *Sūrya.*[31] It is certainly surprising, one must admit, to find a *Sūrya* image in a place where we would naturally look for an *avatāra* of *Viṣṇu.* But, the fact can easily be reconciled if we would only bear in mind the very intimate relation of *Viṣṇu* with the Vedic *Sūrya.* For, there in the *Vedas,* he is never a supreme god, but is always 'identified with the Sun and is said to have stridden over the seven regions and to have covered the whole universe by means of the three steps,'—a statement wherein the germ of the later *Trivikrama* tradition of *Viṣṇu* is so often traced. The idea underlying this solar explanation is obviously incorporated in the *dhyāna śloka*—

> *"Dhyeyas-sadā Savitṛmaṇḍala-madhyavartī Nārāyaṇaḥ sarasijāsana-sanniviṣṭaḥ keyūravān makara-kuṇḍalavān kīrīṭī hārī hiraṇmaya-vapur dhṛtaśaṅkha-cakraḥ."*

Herein *Viṣṇu* as *Nārāyaṇa* is described as residing in the orb of the Sun. The idea that *Viṣṇu* is the Sun appears to be still maintained in the worship of the Sun as *Sūrya Nārāyaṇa.*[32]

Of the two badly defaced images referred to above, one in most probably a representation of the *Vāmana* or *Trivikrama avtāra* and the other of the *Kalki avatāra* of *Viṣṇu.* The former (fig. 15) which is most seriously damaged may be described as standing in a *tribhaṅga* pose on a pedestal which is undoubtedly what remains of a full-blown lotus flower. The right leg is bent almost at right angles at the knee-joint, and the left one is placed firmly on the ground. The deity seems to have only two hands the right of which holds a *kamaṇḍalu* and a staff-like object on which the god seems to lean. The attribute in the left cannot be distinguished. The dress seems to have consisted of a loin-cloth *(kaupīna)* and a waistband which hangs from a knot along side the left hip. But the attributes that give clue to the identification of the image as *Vāmana* or *Trivikrama* is the *kamaṇḍalu* alone referred to above, and the tuft of hair as well tied up in a knot on the crown of the head. For, the canons (*e.g.*, the *Vaikhānasāgama)* would lay down that a *Trivikrama* image should be represented as having two arms, "one of which should carry a *kamaṇḍalu* and the other an umbrella. On the crowns of the head there should be a tuft of hair, tied up in a knot; and there should also be a pair of *kuṇḍalas* in the ears, a deer-skin worn in the *upavīta* fashion, the sacred thread, a waist-zone and a *kaupīna.* He should also carry with him a book. All these are intended to show that the image is that of a Vedic student or Brahmanical *brahmacārin.*" Some authorities hold that the image should be represented as a "deformed dwarf; and they, therefore, require that the image should be worked in the form of an ill-shaped man with hunch-back, protruding joints of bones and a big belly."[33] The image under consideration, deformed and dwarfish as it is, and wearing as it does a *kaupīna*, holding a *kamaṇḍalu* as an attribute, and, finally, having a tuft of hair tied in a knot on the head, seems roughly to agree with both the descriptions. It is likely that he carried a book as another attribute in his left hand.

The other one, we have already surmised, is *Kalki* (fig. 16). It can be described as a standing image with two hands holding in the right a *khaḍga* and in the left some indistinguishable attribute. It has the usual head-dress, heavy ear-ornaments, a heavy necklace and a loin-cloth whose folds can easily be seen. According to the *Agni-purāṇa, Kalki* should ride on a horse and carry the *dhanus* and the *bāṇa* but the *Vaikhānasāgama* states that he should have the face of a horse and the body of a man with four hands carrying respectively the *śaṅkha,* the *cakra,* the *khaḍga* and the *kheṭaka.* Here, the image neither rides a horse, nor has the face of a horse. The only distinguishable attribute in one of his two hands, and on which the identification rests, is the *khaḍaga;* it is not impossible that the left hand carried a *kheṭaka or* shield. And once we have made sure of the identifications of six of the ten *avatāras* of *Viṣṇu,* namely, the *Buddha,* the *Varāha,* the *Narasiṁha,* the *Rāmacandra,* the *Paraśurāma* and the *Trivikrama,* and when the present one is not obviously an image of any of the three other remaining *avatāras* of *Viṣṇu,* namely, the *Matsya,* the *Kūrma,* or the *Kṛṣṇa,* we are led by a process of elimination to identify the present icon as the *Kalki avatāra* of *Viṣṇu.* We can also, therefore, assert in the same breath that the three niches that are at present empty must have once sheltered the images of the *Matsya, Kūrma* and *Kṛṣṇa avatāras* of the most important god of the Hindu Triad.

Besides the Viṣṇuite images of the *Nāt-hlaung kyaung,* a bronze *Viṣṇu* image, one foot high, had been discovered at Pagan by a *phoongyi* (Buddhist monk) in a field at Myinkaba (a village near Pagan) which is at present housed in the Pagan Museum[34] (fig. 17). The question would at once arise if the image, small as it is, had really been carried over from the main land by a Brahmanical trader or colonist; and the question is a likely one. But when we consider the stiff rigid modelling of the body, the hard expression of the face, the paucity of ornaments in so late an example (belonging not earlier than the 13th century A.D.), the rough and rigid convention of the different features, and last, but not the least, the conventional curving flame designs at the ends of the two shoulders, so common in Burmese images of a later date, we are led to believe that the image had not been an imported one, but had, on the contrary, been locally cast by an indigenous craftsman in the service of a Brahmanical master. And, if our assumption turns out to be correct, we can at once evaluate its iconographic importance. The god stands on a double-petalled lotus pedestal and is crowned on the head by a conical *Kirīṭa mukuṭa* finished at the top by a round object, obviously a misrepresentation of the *kirīṭa mukuta* itself. The distended ear-lobes, a characteristic feature of Buddha images, are noteworthy, and the simple and crude workmanship of the ornaments is interesting. The god has four hands, the two upper hold the *cakra* and the *śaṅkha* respectively; the lower right is in the *varada* pose and the lower left is placed upon a staff-like object, obviously the *gadā*. The *yajñopavīta* or the sacred thread across the body is easily recognisable, but interesting is the *udarabandha* or the belt round the belly. This seems frankly to be a *bhogasthānaka mūtri* of *Viṣṇu*, and can well be compared, from the iconographic standpoint, with an exactly similar bronze image from the Madras Museum, illustrated in Gopinath Rao's Hindu Iconography.[35]

These, then, seem almost to exhaust the finds up till now made of Viṣṇuite images in Burma proper. We have seen that they have mostly been found at Hmawza, Thātoñ and deltaic districts in Lower Burma and at Pagan in Upper Burma. It is most unfortunate that none of these images can precisely be dated on any epigraphic evidence. We have, therefore, to fall back upon less precise a data; namely, the stylistic peculiarities of the images themselves, a consideration which we propose to reserve for a later chapter. Here it would suffice to outline in short the period to which these images may possibly be assigned.

The three images from Hmawza belong frankly to two distinct schools. Figures Nos. 3 and 4 are products entirely of a local school by local artists in the employment of Indian masters; and belong, most probably, to a period not earlier than the eighth but not later than the ninth century A.D., when Hmawza or Prome was being ruled by kings of Indian dynasties mentioned in epigraphic records as the *Vikramas* and *Varmans*. Figure No. 2 which shows an artistic combination of Indian and local elements and is undoubtedly one of the best of the early stone sculptures found in Burma, seem to belong on stylistic grounds to an earlier period, most probably to the first half of the eighth century A.D. The two examples from Thātoñ, now housed in the Rangoon Museum, are decidedly Indian in form and composition as also in execution, done no doubt locally by Indian artists, or by artists trained under Indian masters. They seem to have very intimate artistic affinities with the most recent finds of Brahmanical and Mahayanist divinities from Orissa by Rai Ramaprasad Chanda Bahadur, B.A., F.A.S.B., Superintendent, Archaeological Section, Indian Museum, Calcutta, and now housed in the building of the Museum (Exhibits Nos. 28/N.S.2062, 34/N.S.2263, 36/N.S.2264). They seem, therefore, to belong to about the 9th-10th centuries A.D. The sculptures in the *Nāt-hlaung kyaung*, Pagan, seem, on stylistic as well as epigraphic evidence referred to above, to date in the later half of the 11th century A.D. The bronze image must certainly belong to a period not earlier than the later half of the 13th century A.D. To the next century, or probably to a little later date, we may ascribe the stone *Viṣṇu* image from Mergui in the Rangoon Museum. Considered from the viewpoint of these finds just discussed, it can safely be deduced that Brahmanical influx, mainly Viṣṇuite, into the Peninsula began at least as early as the 7th century A.D. and continued with more or less vigour, and in more or less friendly relation with the main Buddhist population, as late as the 14th century A.D. when it seems to have become restricted to the deltaic districts.

REFERENCES

1. An. Rep. A. S. Burma, 1910, p. 18.
2. *Ep. Birm.*, Vol. I, Part II, p. 90 ff.
3. An. Rep. A. S. Burma, 1923, p. 15 ff. Taungdwin, a town said to have been founded in 857 A.D.(?), was called *Rāmāvati,* after the name of the epic hero *Rāma,* who is recognised in South India as one of the ten incarnations of *Viṣṇu.*
4. Ep. Birm., Vol. I, Part II, p. 90; Blagden and Duroiselle.
5. *Ibid.*, pp. 113-15.
6. *Ibid.*, Nos. III-V, pp. 131 and 141 ff.
7. Ep. Birm., Vol. I, Part II, pp. 138-139.
8. Ep. Birm., Vol. III, Pt. I, Mon. Insc., No. I.
9. *Ibid.*, pp. 41-42.
10. Ep. Birm., Vol. III, Part I, p. 44.
11. South Indian Images, p. 70; Krishna Sastri.
12. Exhibits Nos. 23, 24, and 25.
13. Elements Hindu Iconography, Vol. I, Part I, plate LVIII; Gopinath Rao.
14. *Ibid.*, plates XL and XLI.
15. Seated figs. of *Lakṣmī* and *Nārāyaṇa* are frequently seen. See pp. 258-59, *Ibid*, and plate.
16. Phoongyi Kyaung Museum-shed near Hmawza Ry. Station, Exhibit No. 25.
17. "Rūpam," January, 1920.
18. Inventaire Descriptif des monuments Cams, Vol. I, p. 379, fig. 84; H. Parmentier.
19. These two, and a third from Thātoñ which we shall discuss later on in connection with Śaivite images, were brought over to Rangoon where they have found a shelter in the local Government Museum. Exhibits Nos. 8/6, 9/6 and 10/6.
20. An. Rep. A. S. India, 1912-13, p. 136.
21. An. Rep. A. S. Burma, 1902-03, p. 7.
22. Narrative of the Mission to the Court of Ava in 1885, pp. 53 ff.

23. An. Rep. A. S. Burma, 1913, p. 18, plate II, fig. 1.
24. Sculptures aus Pagan by Grünwedel, cited in *An. Rep. A.S. India*, I912-13, p. 136.
25. An. Rep. A. S. India, 1912-13, pp. 136 ff. and footnote, p, 138.
26. An. Rep. A. S. India, 1912-13, p. 138.
27. Elements of Hindu Iconography, Vol. I, Part I, p. 189; G. Rao.
28. *Ibid.*
29. *Ibid.*, p. 186.
30. An. Rep. A. S. India, 1912-13, p. 138; Duroselle.
31. *Cf.* Elements Hindu Iconography, Vol. I, Part II, plates LXXXVI, XCIV (fig. 2), XCVI (fig. 2); G. Rao.
32. *Ibid.*, p. 76; also see, Indian Antiquary, Vol. LIV, 1925, p. 161; J.N. Banerjee.
33. Elements Hindu Iconography, Vol. I, Part I, pp. 163-64; G. Rao.
34. An. Rep. A.S. Burma, 1913, p. 19, para. 47.
35. Elements Hindu Iconography, Vol. I, Part I, plate XVIII; G. Rao.

3 Śiva

The Southern Peninsula of the Indian continent is the favourite cradle of *Śiva*, the third god of the Hindu Triad; and it was most probably from the South that the main stream of the cult flowed towards the colonies where in Campa and Kamboj he commanded the largest following, and occupied an unquestioned supremacy over the two other members of the Trinity. In Campa the two principal groups of temples, namely, those of Mysōn and Pro-nagara, are dedicated to Śaivite gods. He is mentioned in inscriptions as *Maheśvara, Mahādeveśvara, Devadeva, Īśvaradevatā, Īśvaradevādideva*, etc. All these names are such as to signify his predominance over the two other gods. In Kamboj, the first batch of Indian colonists and kings of the early dynasty were, in all probability, Śaivite. *Śiva* or *Maheśvara* thus naturally came to occupy the honoured place of the presiding divinity of the Khmer country. He was known there as *Śiva, Parameśvara, Tryambaka, Girīśa, Jagatpati, Rudra, Īśāna, Śrī Nikāmeśvara, Śrī Tripura-dahaneśvara, Śrī Kapeśa, Śrī Kaṇṭha*, etc. The worship of the *Liṅgam* too was very popular in both the colonies. In Java and other islands of Insulindia where the Hindus had once planted their colonies, *Śiva* was much less popular, for *Viṣṇu* had there the largest following. *Śiva* is nevertheless sometimes mentioned in inscriptions; and images of the god, as well as of his symbolical *Liṅgam*, have come down to us. But it is interesting to note that in the ancient Hindu colony of Siam, which, along with the adjacent colonies of Campa and Kamboj, now forms a part of Indo-China, *Śiva* shared the sane fate as in Java. Stray finds of *Liṅgams*, and of Śaivite gods in stone and bronze have been made from time to time, but their number is limited, and he certainly occupied a less popular position than that of *Viṣṇu.*

In this respect, Burma seems to have been in the same position as Siam. Both the colonies are at present professedly Buddhist, following the Pāli Canon; in both, Brahmanism, nevertheless, found in early times a shelter and claimed a small fraction of the population as its follower; in both *Viṣṇu* seems to have been the most popular god of the Hindu Trinity, and in both, unlike in Campa and Kamboj, *Śiva* was denied an important position by the members of the Brahmanical fold. Temples dedicated to *Śiva* and erected for his worship did certainly exist, as we shall try to show in this chapter, at or near about modern Thātoñ as well as in Pagan; images have also been discovered here and there, coins bearing Śaivite symbols have been found in several districts, especially in Arakan where a Śaivite dynasty of a long line of kings seeing probably to have held sway for a long time; but their number is considerably small and their influence limited. In fact, Brahmanical population in Burma does not seem to have largely subscribed to the cult of *Śiva.*

It has been noticed in the preceding chapter that the Burmese text *Mahayazawin* in describing the story of the foundation of the city of Hmawza or old Prame mentions, along with other divines, the name of *Caṇḍī* and *Parameśvara,* identical with *Devī or Durgā* and *Śiva* or *Maheśvara.* According to the story, *Viṣṇu* presided at the foundation, and he was helped by six other divines, *viz., Gavampati, Indra Nāga, Garuḍa, Caṇḍi* and *Parameśvara,* no doubt suggesting thereby that all these divines including *Caṇḍī* and his lord *Parameśvara,* occupied a position subordinate to that of the supreme god *Viṣṇu.*

In legends and traditions of Burma, *Śiva* has hardly any place, nor is he mentioned in epigraphic records. But numismatic evidence shows that Arakan, the hilly buffer region between the eastern frontiers of India and Burma, had once bean a stronghold of Śaivism, or was at least under the sway of a dynasty of Śaivite kings. Here have been and are still being discovered coins bearing Śaivite symbols, *viz.*, the trident of *Śiva* on the reverse and a recumbent humped bull on the obverse. These coins discovered at different times and at different localities have a family likeness in as much as they all have common symbols; and on the obverse face over the recumbent bull is invariably the legend or name of the king. All these names end with the surname *"Candra,"* and this surname was adapted by at least two lines of kings ruling at Arakan, known as the *Candra* dynasty in local legendary history.[1] Names of a number of *Candra* kings have also been deciphered on a *nāgarī* stone inscription found at the *Shittaung* pagoda, Mrobaung, and dated palaeographically in the 9th-10th century A.D.[2] The coins referred to above, may, likewise, on palaeographic grounds be said to range over a period extending from about the middle of the 4th to the 10th century A.D.,[3] the majority of them, in fact, belonging to the closing centuries. Figures 18a, 18b and 18c are illustrations of coins referred to above having on their obverse the figure of a recumbent humped bull with legend above in *nāgarī* characters, and on the reverse the trident of *Śiva* with garlands pendent from the outer blades. On the reverse face of some of them symbols of the sun and moon can be traced. The *nāgarī* legend can respectively be read as *Vammacandra, Prīticandra, Pṛticandra* and *Vīracandra.*[4] The names are obviously Indian and the symbols Śaivite. It is thus reasonable to conjecture that the *Candra* dynasty of kings of Arakan who ruled from *c.* 400 A.D. to *c.* 1000 A.D. belonged, to the Brahmanical fold and were evidently followers of the cult of *Śiva.*

Coins bearing Viṣṇuite symbols on one side and Śaivite

on the other have also been found in Arakan as well as in Burma proper. Figures 19a, 19b, and 19c show on their obverse a conch-shell which is a Viṣṇuite symbol, and on their reverse, a trident, associated invariably with *Śiva*; here is, thus, a blending of the two cults.[5] Col. Phayre is of opinion that "these were cast .... at a time when Hindu (*i.e.*, Brahmanical) doctrines had undermined Buddhism, a state of affairs which may be traced from the history of the country from the sixth century of the Christian era, at intervals until the eighth. These coins probably were not intended for currency; but might be used as armlets by votaries of the doctrines represented by the symbols."[6] There seems, however, to be no justification for such a surmise.

Existence of the, *Liṅga* cult in Burma has often been urged by Mr. Taw Sein Ko, late Superintendent of Archaeology in the Peninsula; but 'no object which can certainly be identified as a *Liṅgam* has yet been discovered in Burma, and what has often been identified as a, *Liṅgam* may very well be of the shape of a *stūpa*.'[7]

Temples and Images

From stylistic point of view the earliest *Śiva* image in Burma proper seems to be the one discovered at Thātoñ (along with two Viṣṇuite stone sculptures described in the preceding chapter) but now housed in the Government Museum, Rangoon. These three sculptures along with a fourth, which has not yet been traced, must have originally formed part of the *Shwezayan* pagoda of Thātoñ. This pagoda, is furnished with four large niches at the four cardinal sides; and their size and measurement is such as exactly to accommodate the large stone slabs, described as coming from Thātoñ, now housed in the Museum just referred to. These niches which had long been empty have now been used to shelter standing slender figures of modern Burmese Buddha statues that seem incoherent and out of place in the large spacious niches wherein they have found their place. But even the *Shwezayan* does not seem to have been the original abode of these gods; and it is pretty certain that there must have once existed at Thātoñ Hindu dedicated to the worship of these gods, *Viṣṇu* and *Śiva,* and that when these temples were ruined or wilfully destroyed, the images were carried over and installed at the *Shwezayan* to decorate its walls and niche. For, even a casual observation is sufficient to convince one that they do not serve anything but a decorative purpose there and have nothing to do with the cult for which the *Shwezayan* stands.

The *Shwezayan* is a Buddhist pagoda of the kind so common all over Lower Burma, and was built not earlier than the 14th or 15th century A.D. It is a solid brick masonry structure with a raised square base supporting three pyramidal stages connected with a flight of steps at the east. These steps give access to different ambulatory corridors which are provided with outer railings on one side and vertical walls on the other. On the four walls of the first or lowest pyramidal stage were once embedded square and rectangular stone-reliefs, 50 or 52 in number, of which only 14 or 15 are now extant. Most of these even are partially broken and all of them are in a very bad state of preservation on account of the thick whitewash that is annually applied on them. These rows of stoneslabs are relieved on each side by a large niche in the middle which, in our opinion already recorded, once sheltered the three large bas-reliefs now in the Rangoon Museum along with another not yet traced. The importance of these stone-slabs has scarcely been recognised; no attempt has, in fact, been made to prevent their loss and gradual decay, and nobody has ever tried to identify the subject-matter which these slabs relate. And now, owing to the loss of the large majority of these slabs, the thread of the story has been hopelessly lost and the remaining slabs hardly give any clue to their identification. But it seems certain that they tell no Buddhist legend but one frankly of Brahmanical lore or Paurāṇic mythology, For, two *of* the slabs that remain and that are comparatively well-preserved certainly represent *Śiva* with his trident and *jaṭā-mukuṭa*. Moreover, the artistic affinity of these sculptured panels with the three larger Brahmanical reliefs of the Rangoon Museum (which, we assume, were once sheltered in the niches of the *Shwezayan* along with these slabs) is such as to suggest a common cult-relation between the two. To speak plainly, these slabs could not but be Brahmanical. These, as well as the three bas-reliefs; may on stylistic grounds be dated in the 9th-10th century A.D., whereas the *Shwezayan* can in no way be earlier than the 14th or 15th or even later. It is, therefore, certain that neither the reliefs nor the images have anything to do with the Buddhist temple to which they still belong, and it can, therefore, safely be conjectured that they have hardly anything to do with Buddhism too.

Exactly on the same grounds would we assert that these reliefs as well as the three images referred to above originally belonged to one or more Hindu temples, Viṣṇuite or Śaivite, which must have once existed at Thātoñ, and from where they were removed to the *Shwezayan* where the reliefs are at present sheltered. We now proceed to describe in brief the fourteen relief panels that are still extant. It is unfortunate that we have not been able to identify any of them and, as years will roll by, the slaks will gradually become more and more weathered and indistinct, making the task of identification still more difficult if not entirely impossible.

Slab No. 1. Half of the entire slab is broken, the other half represents at the bottom three female figures in an attitude of prayer; just in front of them a male figure squats on the ground. At the top there is a representation of a human figure with a big tail; this is perhaps *Hanumān*, the monkey-god. It may be noted here that images of *Hanumān* are not unknown in Burma; for, the Rangoon Museum houses at least one stone-slab of irregular shape and sandy-greyish colour depicting in low relief the figure of the monkey-god with his tail raised upwards. This slab was found in the Mergui district. (exhibit No. 3/6).

Slab No. 2. The slab which is very badly corroded represents a king or god seated on a throne before which kneels a human figure, partly broken, in an attitude, of prayer. Before the personage seated on the throne is brought another royal personage or divinity seated on a chariot carried apparently by two persons.

Slab No. 3. This undoubtedly represents *Śiva* seated as if he were kneeling. He holds in his right hand the trident which rests on the palm of his left; and is crowned with his *jaṭā-mukuṭa* on the head.

Slab No. 4. This rectangular slab can lengthwise be divided into two portions. At the top, one male figure, probably a royal personage, is seated in an easy position with his left hand on the left knee which is raised, and the right hand placed upon the chest. Over him is the royal umbrellas, before him is a female figure standing, probably asking a favour. At the bottom is a kneeling lady; in front is an animal, perhaps a horse, before which is a round disc-form object.

Slab No. 5. This again undoubtedly represents. *Śiva* with his trident and is in the same position as in No. 3.

Slab No. 6. This probably represents a sheet of water (a sea or a river) which is suggested by waves upon which a male figure rides a horse. He has an open sword in his left hand before him stands a female figure who is preceded by a dancing male figure who wears a *mukuṭa* or crown and holds a *ḍamaru*.

Slab No. 7. It is an interesting sculpture from, artistic, as well as from iconographic point of view. It represents an elephant, perfectly well modelled and in bold relief, upon; which are seated more than two male and female figures in troubled and excited attitudes. Behind the elephant are two figures, one male and the other female, fighting between themselves. The whole is done in bold relief, the composition is at once logical and convincing, and reminds one of the medieval Orissa reliefs.

Slab No. 8. Only a portion remains of the slab.

Slab No. 9. This is also broken; the portion that remains represents two or three figures, very badly corroded. One of them seems to be a Hindu divinity who wears a crown or *mukuṭa.* He stops, it seems, by the indication of his left band, a chariot of which two-wheels only remain. In front of the divinity kneels a woman.

Slab No. 10. It is a broken piece. A male and a female figure are seated on a throne beneath which is a horse.

Slab No. 11. It represents at the top a chariot drawn by a horse; on the chariot are seated two female figures. At the bottom are several male and female figures seated in different positions.

Slab No. 12. It represents at the top a lady, before whom kneel two other ladies, and stands a third of whom only the lower portion remains. Below is the figure of another lady.

Slab No. 13. It represents a squatting figure with his left hand on the left knee and the right on the chest. He is flanked by two female figures, whose way of dressing the hair and the wearing apparel have close affinites with those of contemporary Orissan sculpture.

Slab No. 14. This slab represents a king or divine seated on a pedestal under a trifoil arch; before him kneel some male and female figures.[8]

Of the three bas-reliefs, now in the Rangoon Museum,

two have already been described in the preceding chapter. We proceed to describe the third (Rangoon Museum exhibit: No. 10/6) which has not yet been identified.

The bas-relief measures 4′ X 2′4″ (fig. 20) and stylistically belong exactly to the same class as the two *Viṣṇu* reliefs from Thātoñ. The sculpture is carved out in bold relief on comparatively hard reddish sandstone and are frankly the work of an Indian colonial artist. In form and spirit as well as features and ornaments, it is decidedly Indian. The composition of the piece shows high technical as well as artistic efficiency and brings out in prominent relief its affinity with the early medieval sculptures from Orissa, especially with those lately discovered from different localities of the province just referred to, by Rai R. P. Chanda, Bahadur, Superintendent, Archaeological Section, Indian Museum, and referred to in the preceding chapter. But no less interesting is the iconography of the relief which is of a rare type, if not uncommon, even on the Indian continent.

It represents a god seated in *līlāsana* on a lotus pedestal with a goddess seated between two arms to his left. In size and proportion she takes a minor place in the slab which is almost wholly occupied by the god himself. That she is his consort admits of no doubt; it is evident from the position of the figure and especially from the attitude of the whole body particularly noticeable in the intimate clasp and embrace of the left arm of the god. Her face is roughly weathered, but her richly embroidered cloth as well as her heavy ornaments in her ears and round her neck and hands are quite clear. The dress of the god is also equally rich, and he too, is profusely decorated with ornaments round his neck, arms, wrists, waist and ankles. He wears a crown from which emerges out the *Jaṭā-mukuṭa*, a headdress especially belonging to Śaivite deities; a halo adds dignity to the divine crown. He holds in his two upper hands raised upwards the trident and what we may describe as the *vajra* respectively, and in his two lower hands, resting on his respective thighs, the rosary (*akṣamālā*) and the *mātuliṅga* fruit. The form of the *vajra* is indeed interesting in as much as it differs from all known forms of this particular attribute. But whether we called it a *vajra* or not, it is certain that the slab represents *Śiva* and his consort *Pārvatī* or *Durgā*. The identification finds further support from the fact that the snake which is associated with *Śiva* hangs downwards from the shoulder of the god, and still further by a representation of the bull Nandī shown under the right foot of the god and of the *mahiṣāsura* or the buffalo-demon shown on the left corner of the slab under the seat of *Pārvatī* who is supposed to have killed it. It may, moreover, be noted that the position and attitude of the two figures have a suggestive similarity with those of the famous *Śiva-Pārvatī* relief at Ellora.[9]

The next important *Śiva* image in Burma is at present housed at the entrance of the Ānanda Museum, Pagan, where it was removed from the *Nāt-hlaung kyaung* (fig. 21). It is about 4 ft. high and is carved out of grey soft sand-stone in bold and round relief. Its form and execution is distinctly South Indian and may on stylistic grounds be dated not earlier than the 12th century A.D. In fact, it is about a century later than the *Nāt-hlaung khaung* images, and is of lesser artistic merit. When Col. Yule visited the *Nāt-hlaung* temple in the third quarter of the last century A.D., he saw lying on the floor of the ruined structure a seated and a standing image;[10] the former was afterwards carried over to Germany where it has now been sheltered in the Berlin Museum. This is the main image of the *Nāt-hlaung* temple and has been described in the preceding chapter. The other one was removed to the Pagan Museum. The statue stands on a lotus pedestal in an erect pose; it has four hands, the two upper raised upwards carries the trident and what we may designate as the *vajra* respectively, while the two lower holds the sword and the mace or *gadā*. The variation of the distribution of these attributes forms an interesting iconographic feature of this sculpture, The *kheṭaka* and the *gadā* that are rarely associated with *Śiva* form here two interesting attributes, and the shape of the *vajra*, so unlike its familiar type is also remarkable. An elaborate *jaṭā-mukuṭa* crowns the head, and richly carved ornaments profusely decorate the body. It is undoubtedly a representation of *Śiva* but its presence in a Viṣṇuite temple is certainly interesting. Mon. Duroiselle has already made the most possible assumption, and one cannot but agree with him when he says that "its presence in a Vaiṣṇavite temple, wherein no other Śaivite images have been found would seem to point out to the existence at Pagan of a Śaivite temple from which it was removed after its destruction or its crumbling to ruin."[11]

Recent discoveries at Pagan have brought to light another Śaivite icon, now sheltered in the local Ānanda Museum (fig. 22). It was found on the river-side near *Shwe-ōnhmin* monastery at Myinpagan and is a large, heavy piece of stone sculpture representing a god seated in *rāja-līlā* attitude on a double-petalled lotus pedestal, on which is placed the right foot of the god. Under this foot and on the right side of the pedestal lies flat the figure of a male, and on the left there is indicated by scratches a sheet-like object which might well be a piece of cloth or skin. Is it the deer-skin associated with *Śiva* ? The god seems clearly to have four hands which are all very badly corroded or broken, so much so, that only the *akṣamālā* or rosary can be distinguished in the lower left. The upper right seems to have held the trident. Of his ornaments the heavy *kuṇḍala* on the ears and the *hāra* round the neck can easily be distinguished. The headdress is peculiar and seems to have a form flattened at the top. The god is undoubtedly *Śiva* and the male figure that lies prostrate under his right foot is the *apasmāra puruṣa* known only in South India as associated With *Śiva*. The relief is in a very bad state of decay; the face is almost wiped off and the modelling of the body has suffered to extreme. But it is not difficult to make out the style of the sculpture which is decidedly Indian, more correctly speaking, Indian that had an independent local development in the Peninsula. The sculpture is worked out in bold and round relief, and the general treatment though not very refined, shows yet a sure hand in chiselling and a keen sense of the Indian form. The body that is a little bulky and the peculiar seating attitude give to the sculpture an atmosphere of ease, peculiar to a class of *Śiva* images well known in India. It seems to belong to a period not later than the 11th century A.D. We have noted that the iconography of the sculpture is South-Indian, but the more interesting is the fact that the art-inspiration, like that of the *Nāt-hlaung* images, seems to have come from the North.

The Rangoon Museum shelters an image described as coming from Tenasserim Township, Mergui. "This locality was under the influence of Cambodia very probably up to the early part of the 14th century A.D. There is some epigraphical evidence of this and Talaing histories incidentally confirm it. It had been, earlier, colonised by the peoples from the South of India. It is the *Lang-Khia-Siou* of the Chinese pilgrims, and no doubt was, earlier still, a part, or dependency, or at least under the influence of the old Kingdom of Fünan, so often mentioned by old Chinese writers, as early as the 3rd century A.D. At that period Chinese envoys to India and Indian envoys to China passed through this part of Burma."[12]

This icon constitutes a pair with the standing *Viṣṇu* image described in the previous chapter. Both are described as coming from the same district; they are similar in form and execution, belong stylistically to exactly the same period, *i.e.*, to the 14th century A.D., and are both carved out of similar pieces of rough porous sand-stone, greyish in colour. Both are frankly late South-Indian in character. The figure measures 1′ 9″ in height, the breadth at the base being 11″; the statue itself is 1′ 3″ high and the pedestal on which it rests 6″. It represents undoubtedly a Hindu god seated on a raised pedestal with his left leg placed on it and the right leg hanging from it and resting on the ground, a position which is strikingly similar to that of the *Viṣṇu* image from Ariyambakam (illustrated on page 21 of South Indian Images by H. Krishna Sastri). The Mergui statue seems to have had two hands of which one only remains, and is crowned on the head with what seems to be a *jaṭā-mukuṭa.* This is the only attribute which may suggest it to be an image of *Śiva*. But the stone is so roughly corroded that we are not even sure if the crown is really a *jaṭa-mukuṭa* or a *kirīṭa-mukuṭa*. The identification of the statue shall, therefore, ever remain open to doubt; but, apparently, it seems to be an image of *Viṣṇu*, an assumption, no doubt, having a support in the fact that exactly similar seated attitude of support is quite common in South India, and one such example we have just referred to.

But earlier than even the earliest of all the images described in this chapter, and one of the earliest in Burma, is the fragment of a stone sculpture, distinctly Śaivite in cult and iconography has been discovered. from the ancient site of Wesali in Arakan, a locality where Gupta finds have frequently been made. It forms the lower part of a sculpture and is much damaged. The fragment most probably represents *Durga* in the act of slaying the buffalo-demon or *Mahiṣāsura* (fig. 23) . "The principal figure, the lower half of which only has been preserved, is standing on a lotus with her right foot and a part of her trident resting on the demon.

The demon itself which can scarcely be distinguished owing to its damaged condition is lying prostrate below. It is probably of Gupta date;"[13] more correctly speaking, it belongs to the later Gupta period.

These, then, are the few finds of Śaivite images up till now discovered in Burma. Stray and very few as these finds are, and much removed in date from one another, ranging from the 6th or 7th century A.D. to the 14th the conclusion inevitably follows that they point to the existence of one or more floating mercantile populations who brought their cult and religion with them and had their images locally made for worship. There is no reason or evidence to suppose that they were ever worshipped, by the people as a whole, or to hold that Śaivism had ever been: the religion of the people or of the State, except in Arakan where a Śaivite dynasty seems to have held sway at least for five centuries, from the 5th to the 10th century A.D. This is amply testified to by the coins discovered there as well as probably by the find of the fragmentary slab (fig. 23) described above; which in all probability, is a product of the art and cult patronised by the contemporary Śaivite ruling dynasty.

REFERENCES

1. Phayre, Coins of Arakan, Pegu and Burma, p. 40 (figs. Nos. 9-17) and p. 42 (figs. Nos. 1-9).
2. An. Rep. A. S. Burma, 1926, p. 28.
3. *Ibid.*, 1926, p. 30.
4. Coins of Arakan, Pegu and Burma, Plate II, Nos. 1, 2, 4 and 8; pp. 28-29.
5. *Ibid.*, Plate V, Nos. 6 and 7, p. 33.
6. *Ibid.*, *p.* 33.
7. An. Rep. A. S. Burma, 1924, p. 24; An. Rep. A. S. India, 1910-11, pp. 90-92.

   But quite recently has been discovered at Kalaganōn near Hmawza, a fragment of a stone-slab representing a *Liṅgam* (14" in height), 'an indisputable proof of the existence of Śaivism at Prome side by side with Vaiṣṇavism and Buddhism' (*An. Rep. A.S. India*, 1926-27, p. 182).

8. These slabs have never been photographed. During one of my visits there, I attempted to take photos of some of them; but the whitewash is so thick and they have so roughly been handled that it was difficult to get a good result.
9. Coomaraswamy, Indian and Indonesian Art, see Plate LV, fig. 193.
10. Yule, "Mission to the Court of Ava, 1855," pp. 53-54; An. Rep. A.S. Burma, 1913, p. 19.
11. *Ibid., An. Rep. A. S. Burma*, p. 19.
12. *An. Rep. A. S. Burma*, 1917, p. 19.
13. *Ibid.*, 1916, p. 35.

4 Brahmā and Other Minor Gods

Brahmā

Brahmā, the first god of the Brahmanical Trinity, has been able to command very little influence in Burma. He seems to have had no temple and, as an independent deity, very few adherents too. He has been represented, as we have seen, with *Viṣṇu* and *Śiva* on the *Anantaśayyā* reliefs from Thātoñ and Hmawza; but independent images of *Brahmā* are rare, and only five or six extant examples are known. Of the more interesting of them, one is at present housed in the Rangoon Museum, another is in the Pagan Museum and a third is represented in low relief on the face of the interior pillars of the *Manuha* temple, Pagan. Broken fragments of images of *Brahmā* have here and there been found, for example, in the ruins of the *Zegu* pagoda, Hmawza,[1] as well as at the precincts of the *Shwesandaw* pagoda, Pagan, but even such finds are rare.

The Rangoon Museum *Brahmā* (fig. 29) [2] is carved in bold and round relief out of a rectangular (about 1′4″ × 1′) slab of soft greyish sand-stone. *Brahmā* is seated in *padmāsana* with folded hands raised up to chest-height, a position which, most probably, shows him in an attitude of worship of, or of prayer to, a superior deity. He is represented with three heads with matted locks of hair beautifully dressed in the *jaṭā-mukuṭa* fashion crowned over with a floral ornament.

The Pagan Museum *Brahmā*[3] (fig. 28) conforms exactly to the same description. He is similarly seated in *padamāsana* with folded hands in an attitude of worship; and his three heads are crowned with his matted locks beautifully dressed. But the quality of the stone is better in the present example and the two belong to the strictly different schools. Moreover, stylistically judged, they are separated from one another by a gulf of at least two centuries. The former is the product of a local school of art which is but obvious in the comparatively stiff modelling of the body, in the too much boneless flexible. lines of the different limbs, in the rigid pose and; last but not the least, in the quaint expression of the face. The local artist tutored by his Indian master seems to have worked out an Indian type. But the latter is undoubtedly the product of an Indian artist who gives evidence of his, art and skill in the soft modelling of the body, in the pleasing graceful lines and curves of the limbs, in the most easy position of the body and lastly in the soft pleasing, expression of the face. The sculpture at once reminds one of similar Indian examples of the late Gupta art, traditions of Eastern India; and belongs to a date not later than the 10th century, whereas the Rangoon Museum example seems to be a local product of the 12th-13th century of the Christian era.[4]

There are four images of *Brahmā* carved in very low relief on the faces of the interior square pillars of the *Nanpaya* temple at Pagan. This temple is traditionally known to have been the residential house of the defeated. Talaing King Manuha, who was brought from Thātoñ and kept a captive at Pagan by Anawrahta. Manuha built a temple where a huge recumbent image of the Buddha in his *parinirvāṇa* can be seen, and also a second one just adjacent to the first to shelter himself. These two-temples are situated at Myinpagan and are in a good state of preservation. Curiously enough, the smaller one, *i.e.*, the temple that was used for the residence of Manuha, a king fervently devoted to Buddhism, contains on its pillars images of *Brahmā* carved and modelled in very low and flat relief. The main sanctum of the temple is now empty, and it is difficult to determine whether it was a Hindu or Buddhist deity that was worshipped there. It is not improbable that an image of Buddha himself was installed there at the sanctum to whom the four *Brahmā* images were represented in prayer or worship. Even then, the existence of a Brahmanical deity in the residential palace of a devout. Buddhist shows that the captive king had a decided Hindu leaning.

Herein *Brahmā* is seated on a full blown lotus seat that shoots off its delicately and richly carved stems with leaves and flowers, a beautiful vegetable decoration of considerable artistic merit on two sides of the seated image. *Brahmā* seems to have a soft and flabby body resting on his legs the left one of which is in a squatting position and the right lifted in an angle—a position that is suggestively analogous to what is technically known as *līlāsana.* Unlike the images of *Brahmā* noticed above, here the two hands are not clasped in prayer, but are raised upwards and hold two lotus flowers. The matted locks of hair are arranged in a beautiful *jaṭā-mukuṭa* consisting of carefully intertwined plaits curling capriciously and coquettishly. He has also a halo round his head and a sacred thread, treated in a flat, plastic volume, hanging from his left shoulder. The four images belong to the same type and conform exactly to the same description; but the type itself is interesting for; the lotus attribute in the hands and the particular seated attitude of the god are unique features rarely seen in extant images of *Brahmā.*

Gaṇeśa

A subsidiary deity of the Hindu pantheon, and universally recognised as the remover of obstacles, *Gaṇeśa* or *Vighneśa* easily found favour with the commercial section of the Brahmanical population in India. When Indian traders and merchants began to move towards the countries beyond the seas in the wake of trade and commerce, it was natural that they would take with, them their favourite god as well. It was exactly what happened, for, everywhere in the colonies, *Gaṇeśa* found popular favour mainly with the commercial section of the population. In Burma, especially in the deltaic regions, where the Indian colonists had naturally their commercial stronghold, small images of *Gaṇeśa*, more or less roughly executed, have been found in considerable number. They are all of a very modest size, and crude in execution, and have scarcely any claim to aesthetic consideration. These images, small as they were, were probably meant to be carried from place to place with the individual trader-colonist or the floating company to which they belonged.

The Rangoon Museum shelters two images of *Gaṇeśa*, both roughly worked in low relief, one out of a slab of greyish sand-stone of irregular form, and the other out of a poor specimen of blackish stone, rectangular in form. The former has in elephant-head and a human body with a bulging belly. He is represented as if dancing on his two slim legs, but is really seated. The two upper hands hold what seems to be a *cakra* (discus) and noose, while the two lower hold the *vilva* fruit and the trunk respectively. The latter, also with a bulging belly, is seated in *padmāsana* and has six hands, but the attributes can hardly be ascertained. The upper left seems to hold a trident, the middle right is placed on the pedestal, the lower right holds the trunk and the lower left is placed on his lap. In both instances the figures are so small (about 1′4″ × 1′ and 8″ × 4″ respectively) and the workmanship is so rough that they have nothing but a passing historical and iconographic interest. The assumption is, therefore, natural that these images were used as objects of worship by the readers and commercial section of the Indian colonists who carried their gods along with their merchandise.

I have seen fragments of images of *Gaṇeśa* within the precincts of the *Shwesandaw* pagoda, Pagan, where they along with other Hindu divinities were placed at the corners of the different pyramidal stages as guardian deities of the Buddhist shrine. From an artistic point of view, they mainly served a decorative purpose, as well as *'pieces de accent'* of stone against the brick-setting. But a most interesting *Gaṇeśa* image had lately been picked up from the *debris* of ruins of one of the temples of Pagan (figs. 27a, 27b, 27c).

The whole stele is only 6.5 inches and the image itself 5.5 inches in height; and the material is not stone but white cement plaster. The god is seated ins *padmāsana* with his big bulging belly and elephant-head with its usual big ears and long trunk touching the bulging belly. Of the four hands the two upper hold respectively the *śaṅkha* and the trident; the lower right holds the rosary or *akṣamālā*, while the lower left placed just under the bulging belly holds the *vilva* or *mātuliṅga* fruit. But most interesting is the fact that on the front side of the pedestal is carved in very faint relief the figure of a crocodile, and on the right and left a tortoise and fish respectively. All these are aquatic animals, a feature that is indeed unique; for, nowhere, neither in literature nor in extant examples up till now known, do we find any association of *Gaṇeśa* with these aquatic animals.

There is, however, one possible explanation to offer. We have already suggested that *Gaṇeśa* came to be the most favourite god with the commercial people who used to carry with them their favourite deity. It is most likely that this particular image was the personal property of a floating mencantile community at Pagan who had crossed over the sea to Burma from this side of the Bay of Bengal; and as the sea, which they had to cross, was infested with crocodiles, tortoises And other aquatic animals, these sea-farers wanted to propitiate them. It was, therefore, thought advisable to associate them as attributes or associates of their favourite 'god of success.' Our assumption seems to stand on sure grounds when we take into account that the sea with all her mysterious monsters appealed most to the imagination of these sea-faring traders, and it was inevitable that those gods who had some intimate relation with the sea would become most popular with them (notice, for example, the popularity of the *Anantaśayāna Viṣṇu* in Burma). It was also inevitable that they would associate with their god some of the aquatic animals and monsters they knew.

From Pagan, we have two more images of *Gaṇeśa*. They are miniature votive tablets, and are undoubtedly representatives of a multitude of them which must have once existed in Pagan as personal properties of individual traders or merchants or of floating mercantile communities or parties, essentially Brahmanical in creed and religion, who had assembled there at Pagan, the royal capital, in the wake of trade and commerce. One of these two (fig. 25) is carved out of stone, the other is of white plaster (fig. 26), but both are very crudely executed and hopelessly defaced. In the first, the lower right hand of the deity who is seated in *padmāsana* holds the rosary or the *akṣamālā* and touches the ground, the upper right holds the trident, the upper and lower left hold respectively the *śaṅkha* and the *mātuliṅga* fruit. In the second example, the attributes in the four hands are similar; but the deity is not seated; in *padmāsana,* his right leg is rather raised in an angle breaking as it does at the knee.

Once having thus gained a foothold with the help of his commercial patrons, *Gaṇeśa* gradually carved out for himself an important place in the indigenous religion and mythology of the Burmese, and came to be known as *Mahā-pienne,* and, as such, is still worshipped in the Peninsula.

Sūrya

Archaeological discoveries in Burma have brought to

light, up to this, time at least one image that can definitely be identified as *Sūrya*. This image has been discovered on a hill known as *Shin-nge-det-taung*, situated half a mile to the south-east outside the old city walls of the city of *Mrohaung* in Arakan.[5] But, besides this, we have in one of the niches of the *Nāt-hlaung kyaung* another image which we have already identified as *Sūrya;* and our identification rests on assured grounds.[6] These, then, are the two *Sūrya* icons up till now discovered in Burma; but while the *Nāt-hlaung Sūrya* is definitely of the South Indian type, the Mrohaung example is particularly. North Indian, and the two are at least four centuries removed in date from one another, belonging to the 11th and the 7th or 8th century A.D. respectively. The former we have already studied and described in a preceding chapter; here it would suffice to take only a note of it.

The Mrohaung *Sūrya* (fig. 24) does not stand on his two legs resting on a lotus (*cf.* the *Nāt-hlaung Sūrya)* but rides in his chariot drawn by seven horses. The horse in the centre-placed in a horse-shoe-shaped niche faces outwards, and the remaining six, three on each side, are represented as galloping. "The figure of the chariot-driver *(Aruṇa)* is missing. The principal figure is much defaced but enough remains to show that it has two hands both lifted up to the level of the shoulders, each of which carries a circular or round object, the nature of which cannot be ascertained, being mostly broken off. It has a high headdress, large earlobes and a necklace, and is flanked on either side by what remains of a small standing figure which looks like a female. The one on the right is carrying a bow and that on the left, a staff or any arrow. The two small figures probably represent the two goddesses *Uṣā* and *Pratyūṣā*. The interest of the stone lies in its being the first and only one of its kind that has yet been discovered in Arakan or Burma proper."

It is obviously a *Sūrya* image of the Northern variety, the essential features of which are, 'the seven-horsed chariot of *Sūrya* with *Aruṇa* as the driver; the Sun-god with his legs covered, wearing bodice and jewels, with his two hands carrying two full-blown lotuses, his head adorned with *kirīṭa-mukuṭa;* his two male attendants one on each side and two female figures on either side shooting arrows. The figure of the Sun and sometimes the figures of both the male attendants, too, have their feet encased in some sort of leggings. Sometimes the legs of these three figures are left uncarved and sown as inserted in the pedestal or what stands for the chariot.'[8] The Mrohaung image conforms exactly to this description for here too the legs of the Sun-god as well as those of the two goddesses are shown as inserted 'in the pedestal or what stands for the chariot.' Owing to the defaced state of the sculpture, the figure of *Aruṇa* the driver is missing, but the two full-clown lotuses held in the hands of the, main god as well as the *kirīṭā-mukuṭa* on the head are almost certain. This image is important from another respect too. It supplies us with at least another instance of the Northern type of *Sūrya* belonging to a period of which only one or two examples have up till now come down to us in India. The reason is obvious, for all *Sūrya* images and temples, to which, references are made in Gupta epigraphs seem, with one or two exceptions, to have been lost or destroyed beyond recovery. The earliest *Sūrya* image up till now known of the Northern type is definitely of the Gupta school and cannot be dated later than the 6th century A.D.; it comes from the *Śiva* temple of Bhumārā.[9]

A more or less definite date can be assigned to our sculpture as well. The reverse face of the stele contains a Sanskrit inscription which, unfortunately, is very much disfigured. The palaeography of the record dates it in the earlier half of the 8th century A.D., and the palaeographic evidence is borne out by a stylistic consideration of the sculpture itself which unmistakably bears the stamp of the late Gupta tradition of art. Such sculptures with a strong later Gupta influence have often been discovered in Arakan, and a considerable number of them are Brahmanical.[10] The present example affords an additional and convincing evidence.

REFERENCES

1. An. Rep. A.S. Burma, 1908; p. 6. There is housed in the Rangoon Museum a rectangular stone-slab representing twelve 'seated figures of Brahmanical deities of whom *Brahmā* and *Gaṇeśa* alone are recognisable. Exhibit No. 6/6.
2. Rangoon Museum Exhibit no. 5/6.
3. Pagan Museum Exhibit No. V/74.
4. On the walls of the *Thein-mazi* temple, Pagan, built about the 11th-12th century A.D. there have been discovered wall-paintings depicting, it is asserted, scenes from Buddhist and Brahmanical (?) mythology. One of the characters that form the subject-matter of these paintings, has been sought to be identified as *Brahmā.* Mr. Taw Sein Ko, late Superintendent, Archaeological Survey, Burma, says on page 30 of his Report of the year 1919 : "The figure represented is probably a *Brahmā* of the *Brahmaloka* going through the clouds while being seated in an attitude of adoration. He is on a pilgrimage to the worship at the above shrine. He wears a crown surmounted by a high peak which is surrounded by six lower ones, and has four eyes, two noses and two mouths, and holds conical flowers...... The nose is high, pointed and aquiline, and is distinctly Pyu." We do not see our way to agree with Mr. Taw Sein Ko in identifying this figure as *Brahmā.* Neither his attributes are here seen, nor has he the four faces (three faces are, in fact, represented) by which he is well-known. It might as well be a *Mahāyāna* deity.
5. An. Rep. A.S. Burma, 1923, 27-28, plate 1. fig. 1.
6. Chap. II, plate X, fig. 14.
7. *Op. cit.*, An. Rep. A.S. Burma, 1923, pp. 27-28.
8. *Ind.* Ant., 1925, p. 164.
9. Banerji, Śiva Temple of Bhumārā, *A.S. Memoir*, No. 16, plate XIV, fig. a.
10. *Op. cit.*, An. Rep. A.S. Burma, 1923, pp. 28-29, plate 1, figs. 1, 2 and 3. All these sculptures betray a strong Indian influence of an art tradition

which must have been carried to Arakan by the Indian settlers there. In connection with the Mrohaung *Sūrya* image, Mon. Duroiselle remarks: "It affords an irrecusable evidence of strong Hindu influence in early times in Arakan and of an early Indian settlement at Mrohaung or in its vicinity. In fact, there were found there on Wuntitaung, a hill situated close to the above, remains of a Hindu temple and of Hindu gods, among which may be noticed some Viṣṇuite ones" (*op. cit.*, An. Rep. A.S. Burma, 1923, p. 28). But these images cannot now be traced,

5 Art and Historical Background

I

The images we have studied and described in the preceding chapters may conveniently be assigned to three different periods of artistic activity. First of all we have, as usual, an early period comprising roughly the 7th, 8th and 9th centuries A.D., to which we may assign the *Devī* and the *Sūrya* images from *Arakan,* as well as the *Viṣṇu-Lakṣmī* and two other slabs (Hmawza Museum, Ex. Nos.. 24 and 25) from Hmawza. There is then a medieval period extending from the 9th and 10th to the 12th and 13th centuries of the Christian era. To this period, a period rich in Indian colonial adventure, may be said to belong the three larger bas-reliefs as well as the smaller slabs from Thātōn. The images in the *Nāt-hlaung kyaung* the *Śiva* statue in the Pagan Museum and other images found at or near Pagan, all may be assigned, more or less precisely, to the same period. Lastly we may talk of a late or decadent period comprising the 14th and 15th centuries to which the Tennasserim finds may be assigned; but it is more or less a fiction, for these finds, very few in number, are confined to the deltaic districts and do not seem to be products of any local artistic activity.

Brahmanical as all these images are, it is only too natural to infer that the artistic tradition responsible for them is essentially Indian. Such, indeed, it is; but deeper have we to dive to discover the affinity and influence of particular schools and periods of Indian art which might have been responsible for their inspiration. We have to begin with the Arakan images which we consider to be the earliest in Burma.

The two Arakan images studied in these pages are so badly defaced and mutilated that it is difficult to make a correct consideration of their artistic peculiarities (figs. 23 and 24). But our task becomes somewhat easier if we admit into our consideration two other stone sculptures, one representing a *Nāga* king, and another a *Deva* belonging to the same period and coming from almost the same locality, namely, from the ruins of the *Mahāmuni* pagoda, Arakan (for illustrations of these two sculptures, see plate 1, An. Rep. A. S. Burma., 1923). We have already remarked that they bear on them a distinct stamp what we call late Gupta tradition, of art. The physiognomy of the face of the *Nāga* king and the *Deva* referred to above, the misunderstood position of their feet, and the head-dresses that crown their head are distinctly local; but the soft and lively modelling of their body, the pleasing curves of their face and arms and their sympathetic response in the curves of their ornaments, the easy flow of their lines that glide softly over the hard stone, and lastly, their composition that is at once pleasing arid convincing leave no scope for doubt as to their source of inspiration. And what is easily noticed on these two sculptures is equally present and cab be made out, though with difficulty; on the *Sūrya* and the *Devī* images too Portions of the body that are intact, distinctly show the, same convincing character of its composition, the same soft and lively modelling, and easy flow of lines which are rich and abiding legacies of the Gupta tradition of art. But the exquisitely feminine grace as well as the most subtle and sensitive modelling of the early period of that school are missing in them. This is exactly what it should be, and it helps us to place the Arakan sculptures in a line with the later Gupta sculptures of the 7th and 8th centuries A.D., examples of which are abundant in Eastern India and Assam.

Another remarkable sculpture from the artistic point of view is the *Viṣṇu-Lakṣmi* slab from Hmawza (fig. 2) belonging to a period not later than the 8th century A.D. This finely and delicately modelled sculpture has apparently the grace and softness of a Gupta example; but a closer analysis would show that its source of inspiration is not the one that is responsible for the Arakan images. In fact it owes its existence to a different school of art on this side of the Bay, namely, the Pallava School, and has; consequently, those Gupta features in its form and execution that are inherent in the Pallava School. The most attesting feature of this sculpture is the elongated appearance of the two figures and their supple but bold and rounded legs end aims with their bones and muscles so suppressed as to provide them with a soft grace coupled with a dignified compospre, These characteristics, as well as a consideration of their physiognomical features and of the relation of their body and garments, cannot but suggest a very close affinity with the Pallava tradition of art.

It is most likely, and a careful artistic consideration leads us more to infer that these sculptures were works of Indian artists who had come over to the Peninsula along with Indian traders or priests or colonists in pursuit of their respective vocations of life. But side by side there was also a local artistic activity fostered, no doubt; by the Indian masters. These local artists; who are responsible for many Buddhist images of atone and terracotta that have come down to us, must have also been entrusted with the task of executing Brahmanical images exampler of which have survived to this day. At least two such examples are known from Hmawza (figs. 3 and 4). The very crude and rough execution of an Indian subject-matter, the physiognomy of their faces, the quaint expression of a foolish smile on their lips and not the least, the dress of the divinity standing on his *vāhana Garuḍa* have all combined to give an unIndian character to their appearance. The treatment of the subject-matter is equally foreign to any known school or period of Indian art; the rigid lines and the sharp angularities, the incoherent composition, the schematic surface-treatment of the reliefs and not the least the soulless and meaningless decorations on them are all responsible for the lifeless, almost wooden, atmosphere in which they live. They are mere translations of a canonical text. But here and there cling faint traces, *e.g.*, in the modelling of the body and treatment of the face of the standing *Viṣṇu*, the lessons they received at the feet of their Indian teachers.

The three Thātoñ bas-reliefs as well as the smaller slabs of atone described in a preceding chapter belong to what we may call the mediaeval period. The three larger slabs have attained different standards of artistic excellence and it is most likely that they were executed by different artists, but it seems certain that they belong to the same school of art and the same period of artistic activity comprising roughly the 9th and 10th centuries A.D. In the two *Viṣṇu* reliefs the subject-matter is the same and their iconographic representation is practically of the same kind, but there is considerable difference in their artistic treatment. The larger relief is very badly corroded, but it is not very difficult to ascertain that the modelling of the individual figures of both the reliefs is of the same quality; the treatment of the volume by a schematic arrangement of the figures as well as the general linear composition of the reliefs also differ very little. But it is in the treatment of the surface that the main difference lies. The smaller slab is divided into three, strictly speaking four distinct parallel surfaces schematically arranged and each carved individually almost on the same plane and in comparatively less bold relief with the result that there is hardly any scope for the display of light and shade. It is the treatment of the volume that sets apart each individual surface, not a skilful distribution of light and shade. There is very little scope for contrast in the carving of the different planes of the relief, and the eyes glide from one surface to another slowly and smoothly. But the larger relief at once convinces one of the more technical artistic efficiency of the artist. His sure chisel has been able to carve in different plats and each plane in comparatively bolder relief, and no opportunity has he missed to distribute his larger surfaces on the different planes into as many smaller ones as he could. He has used his subject-matter in a most intelligent and therefore artistic form by introducing elements which he could well leave out. This is evident in the representation of water suggested by lilies and lotuses carved on a lower plane of the relief which on the smaller slab has been left bare. A comparison of the surface-treat of the two reliefs is still better seen in the representation of the lotus-seats (*padmāsana*); on the smaller slab the petals are arranged in one surface and are indicated almost in outlines, while on the larger one the petals are arranged in a double surface and indicated in separate boldly carved petals. The attitude of the two artists is best seen in the comparative treatment of the uppermost portion of the smaller relief and the lowermost portion (*i.e.*, the pedestal) of the larger relief. On the former, the volume of stone has been distributed in three lots carved steles left bare. Such a treatment the artist of the larger relief could never tolerate; this is evident from the fact that he has not even suffered to leave bare the lowermost portion of his large slab of stone, a portion unclaimed by his subject matter. But artistic consideration has necessitated him to carve it not only in deep square panels displaying a nice systematic contrast of light and shade, but also in long parallel lines. This difference in treatment of the surface alone is responsible for the world of difference in the artistic effect of the two reliefs. Thus, one is neat but schematic, lifeless, mechanical and is, therefore, a mere translation of its subject-matter, the other is more lively, more animated, more resourceful, more pleasing more expressive and is, therefore, entirely a new creation.

But the most artistic of the three reliefs and one of the best examples of medieval relief sculptures in India and Burma is the one that represents *Śiva* seated with his consort *Pārvatī* (fig. 20). The whole stele is occupied by the god alone and *Umā* plays only a minor part throwing herself in the background. But how well-planned though complex is the composition that she merges in the linear arrangement of the two left hands and the leg of her lord. Her head and left hand with a portion of her body is carved on the same plane as that of the body and hands of *Śiva* but the remainder of her whole person shifts itself on a deeper plane in a position that is in rhythmic response with the left-side of the body of the god. The linear composition of the relief is effected mainly by the portion of the four hands and the two legs; and this linear movement regulate the mass that is distributed in three bold surfaces, one at the top comprising the two upper hands and the head, one at the right comprising the two right hands, the right leg and the right side of the body, and a third at the left comprising the left hand, the left leg, the left portion of the body of the god and finally the whole person of the *Devi*. There is another surface that comprises the pedestal containing the lotus design, the bull and the buffalo. These four surfaces, we have already said, have been carved in different planes, all in bold and round reliefs. But most remarkable is the complex linear composition referred to above. The two upper hands raised upwards end in angular curves, we find their happy response in the two hands lowered down in delightful lines and soft curves ending in the supple movement of their figures. The surface comprising the head with its halo and *mukuṭa* comes down to rest on the body up to the waist-zone and then, dividing itself into two, takes a linear movement in two the right one in a sympathetic response with the raised right hand and the left one with the raised lower hand and the pedestal below. Thus, in the soft but bold and masculine modelling of the body, in the distribution of the mass in the very difficult surface-treatment in different complex planes resulting in a rich display of light and shade, and finally in the complex linear composition of the whole relief, this sculpture shows the artistic efficiency of the colonial artists at their very best.

We have already remarked that these three reliefs have a close affinity with those lately discovered by Rai Ramaprasad Chanda, Bahadur from different sites of Orissa and now deposited its the Indian Museum Calcutta. In fact, so remarkable is the affinity that one who is not told of the find-spot and the story of its discovery, is apt at a first study of the *Śiva-Pārvatī* stele to style it as Orissan of the 9th and 10th centuries A.D. Moreover, this particular relief has also a considerable iconographic affinity with a *Śiva-Pārvati* relief (Indian Museum, Ex. No. 33/N.S. 2222) discovered along with the images and reliefs just referred to. In form and appearance, in modelling and composition and in their general treatment and execution, these reliefs at least the *Śiva-Pārvatī* and the larger *Viṣṇu* reliefs, have a striking similarity with the Orisṣan sculptures referred to, and it is difficult to discard our assumption that these are certainly works of artists who had migrated from Orissa, then rich in her art-tradition and general culture.

The *Nāt-hlaung* images undoubtedly belong to the medieval period, but all about a century and a half later than the Thātoñ reliefs. We have already referred to a South Indian Tamil inscription, palaeographically dated in the 13th century A.D. recording the gift by a *Vaiṣṇava* saint, a native of Craganore in Malabar, of a *maṇḍapa* in the temple of

Nānādeśi Vinnagar Alvar at Pagan. "*Nānādeśi Vinnagar*," says Dr. Hultzsch, "means the *Viṣṇu* temple of those coming from various countries. This name shows that the temple, which was situated in the heart of the Buddhist country of Burma, had been founded and was resorted to by *Vaiṣṇavas* from various parts of the Indian Peninsula."[1] Mon. Duroiselle is perhaps right in asserting that the *Vaiṣṇava* temple mentioned in this epigraph refers to the *Nāt-hlaung* temple which he is inclined to assign to the 13th century A.D. But I have tried to show in a previous chapter that the epigraph refers not to the erection of the temple itself, but to a *maṇḍapa* which might well have been added later on. The temple cannot, in our opinion, if we are to judge by the sculptures are its niches as well as by the architectural style, date later than the middle of the eleventh century A.D.

In view of the fact that a Tamil inscription has been discovered in the *debris* of the temple purporting to relate that the temple had been founded and resorted to by *Vaiṣṇavas* from various parts of the Indian Peninsula and that the iconography of some of the images (*e.g.*, the *Sūrya*) are distinctly South Indian, it is only natural to conclude at once that the *Nāt-hlaung* images owe their artistic inspiration to a contemporary South Indian School of art. Had it been so, our problem would have been as easy as one can naturally expect under such circumstances. Unfortunately, such an assumption is not borne out by a careful consideration of the sculptures themselves.

These images are very badly defaced, and it is difficult to make a systematic artistic survey of each individual image. But the general features and characteristics are easily recognisable from what remains of some of them,[2] *e.g.*, the *Kalki*, the *Sūrya*, the *Rāmacandra* and the *Paraśurāma* images. The hard but lively modelling of the body, the regular lines that control the slim arms and legs and the gradual attenuating curve from the chest to the waist broadening itself downwards on the hips, at once turn our eyes and attention to the large number of sculptures of the Eastern School of art of the Pālas and Senas of Bengal and Bihar whose rule comprised the centuries from the 9th to the 12th. Our surprise increases all the more when we consider the physiognomy of the face and the body and discover its close affinity with that of the sculptures of the particular school referred to. They have all slim but well proportioned arms and legs, a broad chest that gradually merges itself in an attenuated waist and a pair of well balanced hips. Their head-dresses and ornaments too are strikingly similar, and it is particularly noticeable in the heavy earrings, arm-lets, wristlets and finally in the fluttering scarves over the two shoulders, a feature that is hardly missed in the Buddhist and Brahmanical images of the Eastern School. But we become almost certain of our assumption when we notice the closest affinity of their facial treatment. It is roundish with a pointed chin, and the two lips, the lower one of which is slightly modelled in a rounded curve, are downwards to give a smile of bliss and contentment. A not very sharp nose finishes itself up into two faintly modelled curves of eye-lashes that give a restful shade to the half closed eyes below and a pointed downward motion to the broad forehead above. Thus from the point between the two eyelashes to the pointed chin there is a downward motion relieved only by the rounded cut of the face. All these are characteristic features of the Eastern School of art revealed in innumerable Buddhist and Brahmanical images found all over the country that comprise the modern provinces of Bihar and Bengal.

Now, it is indeed surprising how in a temple that is supposed to have been built and patronised by *Brāhmaṇas* from South India and where the iconography of the images are South Indian, the images themselves happen to be works belonging to, or deriving their inspiration from a School of Art in Eastern India ? But, howsoever surprising it might be, our finding can scarcely be doubted, and if we are to accept it, the conclusion becomes inevitable that services of artists imported from Eastern India or at least trained in the art-tradition of that particular school must have been requisitioned by the South Indian masters who had most probably been responsible for the building and upkeep of the temple itself.

To this tradition of art, though undoubtedly to an earlier date, must also belong the seated image of *Bramhā* now in the Pagan Museum (fig. 28). The figure is badly damaged, but enough remains to show the soft texture of its modelling, the masculine vigour of the physiognomical form, the bold but graceful lines that regulate the mass, the surface treatment of the face that has delighted in a display of light and shade by means of deep chiselling in bold and logical curves which is responsible for the decidedly Indian expression of the face, and lastly the well balanced, though not original, composition of the whole stele. The facial and the bodily type and the character of the modelling and general treatment take us so near the comparatively early examples of the Eastern School of art that a very close affinity between the two art traditions cannot but very naturally suggest itself.

But these remarks cannot be applicable to the standing *Śiva* image of Pagan, belonging undoubtedly to a period not earlier than the 13th century A.D. Unlike that of the *Nā-haung* images the material of this sculpture is a kind of very soft sand-stone, and the modelling is somewhat hard and stiff. The two arms modelled in the round are heavy and the legs both heavy and static. The pose and composition are conventional and the treatment of the surface does not show any very strong contrast of light and shade. The elaboration of ornamental details which are here conspicuous by their presence is a characteristic feature of late medieval sculptures, and the static heaviness invariably reminds one of late South Indian, especially Cola, exarr.ples with which the present icon has a close affinity.

Regarding the artistic consideration of other minor images, stone or bronze, we have hardly anything to say more than what we have already done in the preceding pages. They have scarcely any artistic justification, and their interest is mainly historical and iconographical. The Tennasserim images, the bronze *Viṣṇu* from Myinkaba, Pagan, and the miniature *Gaṇeśa* and other sculptures are almost all late South Indian, but were in most cases locally cast or carved. They are works not of any particular school or schools of art that flourished. in the Peninsula, but of local craftsmen called to service by South Indian masters who had been there for purposes of trade and commerce.

II

Considered from the view-point of both art and iconography of the images studied and described in these pages, Brahmanical element in Burma seems to have made its mark at leas as early as the 6th century A.D., and continued to have its snare of influence on the people up to at least the 14th. But it should distinctly be understood that this element was more or less confined to the Indian section of the population, and we have as yet no evidence at hand to show that Brahmanism could ever replace Buddhism which was the religion of the state as well as of the people in general. Brahmanism was obviously the religion of the Indian minority who had been given the right of freedom of worship according to their own choice and belief. And as Buddhism in Burma was not exclusive at the beginning, it was possible for some of the Brahmanical gods to be incorporated into their legends *(e.g.,* the *Mahāpienne-Gaṇeśa),* as well as in some of the Buddhist temples as subsidiary deities (*e.g.*, in the *Shwesandaw,* the *Nanpaya,* etc.).

Brahmanical element in Burma during the early days of her history seems to have been confined to Arakan on one side and to Lower Burma, *i.e.*, the kingdom of Hmawza on the other. In Arakan the artists responsible for these images came along with people who had migrated from Eastern India, and at Hmawza, most probably, from the Pallava country, the former, obviously, by the land route and the latter by sea. Arakan, in those days, formed more a part of the Indian frontier than a province of Burma, and relations and intercourse with Bengal and Assam were far more frequent than we can possibly imagine. Numismatic evidence have proved that a Brahmanical dynasty of kings whose names end with *Candra* ruled over Arakan from at least the 5th to about the 11th century A.D.[3] Sanskrit inscriptions Palaeographically dated from the 7th to the 10th century A.D. have been discovered at and near about Mrohaung, the capital city of Arakan, and the script is decidedly of the later Gupta and early Pāla periods.[4] Old Prome, and, as a matter of that, Lower Burma was during the 6th, 7th and 8th centuries of the Christian era dominated by an Indian dynasty of kings known as the Vikrama dynasty.[5] It was most probably under the aegis of this dynasty that Brahmanism made its mark in Lower Burma, and the images discovered at the site of the capital city are no doubt contemporaneous. But it is difficult to ascertain from which part of India this Hinduised dynasty had migrated into the Peninsula. The *Viṣṇu-Lakṣmī* slab shows Pallava affinities but evidence of Pallava relations with Burma are but scanty, though the Indian colonies of Campa and Kamboj, Java, Sumatra and Malay owe much to Pallava enterprise. In fact the earliest epigraphic record found, in

Indo-China is in the early Pallava script, and the monuments of Campa and Java are definite proofs of much that is borrowed from the Pallavas. The Pallavas maintained an active maritime commerce but no evidence has yet been furnished to show any attempt at any systematic colonial or commercial enterprise in this 'land of gold.' There might have been some floating companies planted on the coastal regions of the Peninsula, but they have left very little trace and have hardly left any marked influence on the history of any period of Burmese culture and civilization. But mention must here be made of the discoveries made at Hmawza (old Prome) of two gold plates three fragments of a stone inscription, a small votive *stūpa,* and a gold-leaf manuscript, all bearing Pāli inscriptions in a script very closely allied to the *Canara-Telegu* script of the 5th and 6th centuries A.D.[6] Stone and terracotta sculptures bearing unmistakable traces of Gupta influence have also been discovered in the same locality.

In Thātoñ, *i.e.,* the ancient *Rammaññadeśa,* the land *par excellence* of the Talaings, the Indian, at least the Brahmanical, element was imported decidedly from Orissa, the ancient Odra or Kaliṅga. The ancient name attributed to old Prome is *Śrīkṣetra,* so often mentioned in the Mōn records[7] as *Sikset* or *Srikset,* and by the Chinese pilgrims as *Si-li-cha-ta-lo;* and *Śrīkṣetra* is the holy land of Puri on the ancient Kaliṅga coast. The name *Śrīkṣetra* given to old Prome may be apocryphal; but the attribution itself is significant, however late it may be. The old name for Pegu is *Ussa* which is but a form of Oḍra or Orissa.[8] It is difficult to disbelieve that Pegu was colonised from Orissa or was once dominated over by a people who had migrated from Orissa. Indeed these classical names are but survivals of actual colonisation from the original countries inhabited by the colonists themselves. The later authorities who used those names did not satisfy their whims alone but their remembrances of actual facts as well that constantly harked back to their origins. Lower Burma is the land of a people who were and still are called *'Talaings.'* The term used as early as 1107 A.D. in Mōn records is but a derivation of *'Telingānā'* or *'Trikaliṅga'*, a name used to mean almost the whole of the Andhra. Kaliṅga zone. Likewise, the earliest colonisation of the Malay Peninsula and Java had probably been made from Kaliṅga, for the Hindus of the Peninsula and the island were and are still known as *'Kling.'* Notice should also be taken of the fact that gold coins of the Eastern Cālukya kings have been found in Arakan and Siam. These facts are sufficient to testify to the existence of a very intimate intercourse that existed between the Andhra-Kaliṅga country and the countries beyond the seas. Inscriptions in Eastern Cālukya character have been discovered in Burma, and there are scholars who would think as well that the Talaing script is but a derivation of the Telegu or Andhra-Kaliṅga script. When we consider all these, we must recognise the important role that Andhra-Kaliṅga played in the history of Indian expansion; we must also admit the fact that long before the Pallavas and the Colas contemplated intercourse with lands and peoples on the other side of the Bay, the Kaliṅgas had actually achieved it, at least in Burma, if not anywhere else.

Pagan in Upper Burma, became the mistress of the Burmese world after the conquest of Thātoñ in 1057 A.D. Anawrahta, the first important king of Pagan, came to the throne in 1044 A.D., and with him began a long line of kings who had received and patronised a religion that is still the solace of many souls, and had reared up monuments that have enriched posterity for ever. Her kings, one after another, flung open her doors to outside intercourse within the Peninsula itself and outside as well. It was this intercourse, of Pagan with the outside world that inaugurated the classical period of the history of Burma. Emigrants from all parts of India, Eastern India and Orissa, the Cola country and Ceylon as well as from tyke colonies began to Tour in incessantly in the wake mainly of trade and commerce. Terracotta votive tablets in *nāgarī* characters of the 10th-12th centuries A.D., and inscriptions in Tamil characters of the 13th[9] have been discovered along with images that belong mainly to the medieval Eastern as well as to the Cola Schools of art. Her innumerable monuments, when closely analysed and examined, reveal influences from Bengal on one side and Orissa on the other. Still there are others in which Ceylonese element predominates, and the contribution from the colonies cannot also be left out of consideration. Her Buddhism was Ceylonese, but she drew monks from Bengal who sailed from Tāmralipti, from the Cola country who sailed from Conjeeveram or ancient Kāñchīpuram as well as from Ceylon.[10] It is thus evident that Pagan fostered a culture and civilization very complex in character assimilating with her national genius contributions and influences from all countries and peoples that came in contact with her. This explains why we have to meet with artists from Eastern India or at least trained in that particular school of art employed in a temple most probably reared up and patronised by South Indian *Vaiṣṇavas,* and where the iconography of the gods are undoubtedly South Indian.

But Pagan fell in 1287 A.D. at the deadly blow of the Mongol army of Kublai Khan, and the country sank in chaos and disorder, and never was Burma once more unified under a single central authority. Indian relations with Burma, mainly, commercial, continued to exist for another century and a half but it became strictly confined to the deltaic coasts which explains the discoveries made of some Brahmanical images in Mergui and other deltaic districts. Mutual relations was revived during the reign of Dhammaceti, king of Pegu, in the 15th century A.D., but it was strictly with Ceylon, and the initiative came from the other side of the Bay. No archaeological finds either Brahmanical or Buddhistic, having any characteristic Indian affinity have up till now been discovered anywhere in Burma after the 14th century A.D. and there is, in fact, hardly the possibility of any such discovery.

The reason is obvious. Hindu India that was the fountain of inspiration for all cultural and religious activities in the Peninsula became herself dominated by an alien unsympathetic people, the Muhammadans. After an active and strenuous life of hundreds of years she had exhausted herself, and her culture and civilisation had come down to a very low ebb. Her colonial activities had practically ceased, and the colonies where she had once unfurled her flag of cultural supremacy had gradually come to be overrun by savage tribes from the north—the Shans, the Mongols, the Thais, the Laos, the Annamites and others. Cut off thus from their most vital source of inspiration and activity, they were gradually overpowered by other peoples, races and religions.

But amidst chaos and conquests Burma retained the sacred religion of Buddhism she received from India where it had almost become extinct. Burmese Buddhism, therefore; gradually became strictly exclusive and maintained its relations, when occasion demanded, with Ceylon alone. Burma is still professedly Buddhist an still turns to that sea-girt island to settle all her problems and disputes of religion.

Brahmanism in Burma is, thus, only an episode in the history of early Indo-Burmese relations. It could never take root in the soil, and never could it win over to its side any considerable number of followers. It was mainly confined to the Indian section of the people who had been there chiefly for purposes of trade and commerce or other vocations of life, and it is only natural that these emigrants had their share of influence on the people of the land and the culture reared up on its soil.

REFERENCES

1. An. Rep. A.S. India, 1912-13, pp. 136-37.
2. It is difficult to have satisfactory results from the accompanying illustration. I, therefore, examined the sculptures on the spot and the description that follows is based on a study of the stone sculpture themselves, not of their photos.
3. Coins of Arakan, Pegu and Burma, Phayre, *op. cit.*
4. An. Rep. A.S. Burma, 1923, pp. 27-28 and 1926, p. 28.
5. An. Rep. A.S. Burma, 1924, p. 23. Quite recently has been discovered at Hmawza a line of inscription in Pyu around the lower rim of a votive *stūpa*. The inscription contains two names, *Śrī Prabhuvarma* and *Śri Prabhudevi,* which seem to be the titles of the king then reigning and his queen. The name-ending *Varman* is interesting; for royal titles ending in *Varman* are frequently met with in South Indian History, specially in the dynasty of the Pallavas, as well as in those of some of the colonial Indian royal dynasties of Indo-China and Indonesia (An. Rep. A. S. India, 1926-27, pp. 171 ff.).
6. An. Rep. A.S. Burma, 1924, pp. 21-23.; An. Rep. A.S. India, 1926-27, pp. 171 ff.
7. *Op. Cit.*
8. An. Rep. A. S. Burma, 1923, pp. 15 ff.
9. *Op. cit.*
10. Ep. Birminica, Vol, III, Part II, pp. 190-91.

Bibliography

Original Literature

Amarakośa, with commentary of Rāmāśramī, Bombay, 1915. p. 1915.

Ambāṣṭaka Ānandalaharī by Śaṅkara.

Anyāpadeśaśataka by Nīlakaṇṭha Dīkṣita, see *Minor Works* of Nīlakaṇṭha Dīkṣita and Filliozat.

Arthaśastra by Kautilya, text and trans. 2 vols. Sharma Sastri, Mysore 1924; text. and trans. and Kangle, 3 vols. Boṃbay, 1960-63.

Āryaśataka by Nīlakaṇṭha Diksita, see *Minor Works* of Nīlakaṇṭha Dīkshita and Filliozat.

Atharvaveda, with Sāyaṇa's commentary, 4 vols. Bombay, 1895-98, trans. W.D. Whitney, Harvard Orien Series, 2 vols. Harvard, 1905.

Avadānakalpalatā by Kṣemendra, *Bibliotheca Indica Series*, vols. Calcuttam 1888-1929.

Bhagavadgītā, Gītā Press, Gorakhpur, 1934.

Bhāgavata by Vyāsa, text trans. Gītā Press edn., Gorakhpur, 1971.

Bhāgavata-Purāṇa.

Bhaviṣya Purāṇa, Venkatesvara Press, Bombay, 1910.

Brahmāṇḍa Purāṇa, Venkatesvara Press, Bombay, 1923.

Brāhmīya-Śilpa.

Bṛhatsaṁhiṭa (Varāhamihira).

Chaturvargachintāmani (Hēmādri).

Dakṣiṇamūrtistotra by Śaṅkara.

Devīsūkta see *Ṛgveda.*

Devyoparādhakṣamāpaṇastotra by Śaṅkara.

Dvitrlṁśaputtalika Siṁhasana. Harvard Oriental Series.

Gaṇeśa. Chaukhamba Sanskrit Series, Varanasi.

Gaṇeśavijaya Kāvya Baroda, 1983.

Gāthaspataśati.

Harivaṁṣa by Vyāsa Gītā Press, Gorakhpur.

Harṣa Carita, Bāṇa.

Konakadhārāstava by Śaṅkara.

Kāśyapa-Śilpa (from the Bhānumat or Aṁsumat-Tantra).

Kaṭākṣaśataka by Mūka, see *Mūkapañchaśati.*

Kirātarjunīya by Bhāvari, with Mallinātha's commentary, Bombay, 1907.

Kumārasaṁbhava by Kālidāsa, with the commentary of Mallinātha, Bombay, 1916.

Lalitāssahasranāma see *Brahmāṇḍa Purina.*

Llitāpañcaratna by Śaṅkara.

Lalita Vistara, Gaekwad Oriental Series, No. 53, Baroda. 1959.

Mahābhārata by Vyāsa, Gītā Press edn., Gorakhpur.

Mālati Mādhava of Bhavabhūti, Ed., Sahitya Sudhakara, Varanasi.

Mānasāra.

Manu Smṛti, Poona, 1937.

Mayamata.

Mṛcchkaṭika by Śūdraka, with Pṛthvīdhara's commentary, Bombay, 1922.

Mudrārākṣasa by Viśākhadatta, with the commentary of Dhuṇḍi-rāja, Bombay, 1928.

Navasahasrāṅkacarita of Padmagupta, Chaukhamba Sanskrit Series, Varanasi.

Nilakaṇṭhakavijayachampa by Nīlakaṇṭha Dīkṣita, Śrī *Bālamano-ramā Series*, Madras, 1924.

Nitiśataka by Bhartṛhari, see *Śatakartraya*.

Niśpannayogāvalī.

Padma Purāṇa, Bengal Printing Works, Calcutta, 1959.

Rājatraṅgiṇī of Jonarāja, Chaukhamba Sanskrit Series, 1972.

Sabdakalpadruma (the Encyclopaedia of Sanskrit Literature by Rājā Rādhākānta Deo; printed in Calcutta).

Śatakartraya by Bhartṛhari, Bhāratīya Vidyā Series, Bombay, 1945.

Śilparatna.

Śilpasaṅgraha

Śilpasāra.

Śiśupālavadha of Magha, Ed. Bombay, 1933.

Śivanandalahari by Śaṅkara.

Śivāparādhakṣamāpaṇastotra by Śaṅkara.

Śivokarśamañjarī by Nīlakaṇṭha Dīkṣita, see *Minor Works* of Nīlakaṇṭha Dikṣita and Filliozat.

Skanda Purāṇa, Bombay, 1910.

Śrisūkta.

Sūtasaṁhitā.

Sūryaśataka by Mayūra, Kāvyamāla Series, Bombay, 1887.

Svapnavasavadatta of Bhāsa, Chaukhamba Sanskrit Series, Varanasi.

Araṇyaka, with the commentary of Sāyaṇa, Ānanda- śrama Series, 2 vols., Poona, 1887.

Taittirīya Brahmana with the commentary of Sāyaṇa, Ānandā-śrama Series, Poona, 1930.

Taittirīya Saṁhitā with the commentary of Sāyaṇa, Anandāśrama Series, 8 vols., Poona, 1928, *Tattvanidhi* (with numerous quotations; printed at the Śrī Veṅkateśvara Steam Press, Bombay).

Uttararāmacarita by Bhavabhūti, with the commentary of Vīrarāghava, Bombay, 1919.

Vairāgyaśataka by Bhartṛhari, see *Śatakatraya.*

Vairāgyaśataka by Nīlakaṇṭha Dīkṣita, see Minor Poems of Nīlakaṇṭha Dīkṣita and Filliozat.

Varāha Purāṇa, All India Kashi Raj, Trust, Varanasi.

Vāyu Purāṇa, Ānandāśrama Paṇḍit, Poona, 1983.

Vikramāṅkadevacarita of Bilhaṇa, BHU, Varanasi, 1964.

Yajñavalkya Smṛti, Poona, 1937.

Dharmakośasaṁgraha.

Acharya, P.K., *Viṣṇudharmottara Purāṇa.*

Agrawala, R.C., *Bhāratīya Vidyā, XX-XXI.*

Agrawala, R K., *Architecture of Mānasara, Vol. IV,* (Reprint) Delhi, 1980.

——, A note on the Ardhanārī Gaṇapati, JISOA, IX, (Dr. Motichandra Commemoration Volume, Part-II).

Agrawala, VS., Ed., *Kādambari of Bāṇa,* Varanasi, 1958.

——, Mathura Terracottas, *Journal UP Historical Society,* 2 Lucknow, 1936.

——, *Matsya* Purāṇa—A Study, Varanasi, 1963.

——, *Studies in Indian Art,* Varanasi, 1965.

——, *Vāmana* Purāṇa—A Study, 1964.

Alaxendar, B. and others, Varanasi Seals *and Sealings,* Varanasi, 1963.

Albrecht, Weler, Ed., *Satapatha Brāhmaṇa with commentery of Sāyaṇa,* Alfred Lyall, K.C.B., *Asiatic Studdies* (2 vols.), 1897.

Allen, J., *Catalogue of the Coins of the Gupta Dynasty and of* Śaśāṅka of Garuda, British Museum, London, 1914.

——, *Catalogue of Coins of Ancient India, British* Museum, London, 1936.

Amara Singh, Amarakośa, (Quoted by RV. Kane in the *History of Dharmaśāstra).*

Ananda Krishan, *Malva Paintings,* Varanasi, 1963.

Appuswamy Jaya, *Indian Paintings,* Varanasi, 1963.

Bagchi, P .C., *Studies in Tantra,* Calcutta, 1920.

Bakshi, D.N., *Hindu divinities in Japanese Buddhist Pantheon,* Calcutta, 1979.

Baldeva Upadhyaya, *Agni* Purāṇa, K.S.S., Varanasi, 1966.

Banerjea, *J.N., Development of Hindu Iconography,* Calcutta, 1956.

——, *Purāṇic and Tantric Religion,* Calcutta, 1955.

Banerji, R.D., *Eastern Indian School of Medieval Sculpture,* Delhi, 1933.

——, *The Haihayas of Tripurī and their Monuments,* Calcutta, 1931.

Barnett, D.E., *Sculptures from Amarāvati in the British Museum,* London, 1954.

Barth, A., *The Religions of India,* 1891.

Basil Gray, *Rajput Paintings,* Faber and Faber Ltd.

Bernel, Kempers, *A.J., Ancient Indonesian* Art, Amesterdam, 1958.

Bhandarkar, R.G., Vaiṣṇavism, *Saivism and other Minor Religious Systems,* Satrasburg, 1913.

Bhattacharya, B.C., *The Jain Iconography,* Delhi, 1974.

Bhattacharya, Benoytosh, *Indian Buddhist Iconography,* Calcutta, 1956.

——,Ed., *Sādhanamāla,* Baroda, 1925-28.

Bhattashali, *N.K., Iconography of Buddhist and Brahmanical Sculptures in Dacca Museum,* Dacca, 1929.

Bhisham, Pal, *The Templet of Rajasthan, Jaipur,* 1969.

Bloch, T.L., *Excavations at Hasarh, Arch. Sur. Ind. Ann. Report,* 1903-04.

Bloomfield, Mourice, A *Vedic Concordance,* Harvard Oriental Series, Harvard, 1906.

Bose, P , Indian *Teachers in China,* Madras, 1923.

Briggs, L.P, *The Ancient Khmer Empire,* Philadelphia, 1951.

Chatterjee, Asoka, *Padm—A Study,* Calcutta, 1970.

Chattopadhyaya, Sudhakara, *The Evolution of Theistic Sects in Ancient India,* Calcutta, 1962.

Chhabra, *B.C., Antiquities of Chamber State, II,* Delhi, 1957.

Coleman, *C., Mythology of the Hindus,* London, 1832.

Coomaraswamy, A.K., *History of Indian and Indonesian Art,* London, 1927.

——, *Le Stapa de Bhdrhut, Ars Asiatica,* Paris, 1956.

——, *Yakṣas,* 2 vols., Washington, 1928, 1931.

——, *Early Indian Iconography, Eastern Art,* Philadelphia, 1929.

Cowell, E.B., Jātakas, 6 volumes, Cambridge, 1895-1907.

Crooke, I.C.S., *The Popular Religion and Folk-Lore of Nothern India,* 1896.

Cunningham, A., *Stapa of Bhārhut,* London, 1879.

Davivajna, K.N. *Somaji, Concept of Gaṇeśa,* Bangalore, 1983.

Dawee Daweewarn, *Brahamanism in South East Asia,* New Delhi, 1982.

Deva, K., *Images of Nepal, New* Delhi, 1984.

Downson, J., *A Classical Dictionary of Hindu Mythology,* London, 1903.

Dubois Abbé, J.A., *A Description of the Character, Manners, and Customs of the People of India,* 1862-3.

Dvivedi, S.K., Ed., *Kathāsaritasāgara* of Somadeva, Patna, 1977.

Eden, Pargitar, F, *Mārkeṇḍeya Purāṇa,* Calcutta, 1904.

Edkins, J., *Chinese Buddhism,* London, 1893.

Edward Moor, *The Hindu Pantheon,* 1810.

Edwin Arnold, *The Light of Asia,* 1890.

Eliot, Charles, *Hinduism and Buddhism*, 3 vols. London, 1921, Reprint, Delhi, 1957.

——, *Japanese Buddhism*, London, 1935.

Farquhar, J.N., *A Primer of Hinduism*, 1911.

Fausball, Ed., *Jātakamālā*.

Fergusson, James, Cave *Temples of India*, London, 1880.

——, *Tree and Serpent Worship*, London, 1868.

Feroci, C., *The Siam*, Bangkok, 1967.

Filliozat, PS., Gueres poetiques de Nīlakaṇṭha Dīkṣita, Pondicherry, 1967.

Fleet, J.F., *Gupta* Inscriptions of the Early Kings and their Successors, *Crops. Insc. Ind.* 3, Calcutta, 1888.

Foucher, A., *The Beginning of Buddhist Art*, London, 1917.

——, *Iconographic Buddhiqui de l'India*, Vol. I, Paris, 1900.

Francke, *A.H., Antiquies of Indian Tibet*, A.S.I., Vol. XXXVIII.

Garg, *Ganga Ram, An Encyclopaedia of Indian Literature*, Delhi, 1982.

Gatty, Alice, Gaṇeśa, Delhi, 1971.

Geo, Howells, *The Soul of India*, 1913.

Goetz, Herman, *Art of the World Series, Vol.* I, London, 1960.

Gordon, A.K., *Tibetan Religious Art*, New York, 1963.

Griffith, Ralph J.H., *The Rāmāyaṇa*.

Griswold, Alexander B., *Art of the World Series*, (Burma, Korea and Tibet), Lodon, 1964.

Grunwedel, *Buddhist Art*. Oxford, 1941.

——, *Mythologic Des Buddhismus*, Leipzig, 1900.

Gubernates, *Zoological Mythology*.

Gupta, Ananda Swarup, *Vdinana Purana*, Varanasi, 1968.

Gupta, *R.S., Iconography of Hindu, Buddhists, Jains*, Bombay, 1972, 1980.

Gupta, S.K., *Elephant in Indian Art and Mythology*, Delhi, 1983.

Gupta, Sanjukta, (Tr.), *Lakṣmī Tantra*, Leiden, 1972.

——, (Tr.), *Mahānirvāṇantra*, Leiden, 1972.

——, (Tr.) *Rudrayāmala Tantra*, Leiden, 1972.

——, (Tr.), *Vāmācāri Herambaśūla*, Leiden, 1972.

——, (Tr.), *Vighneśvara Pratiṣṭhā Vidhi*, Leiden, 1972.

Handa, Davendra, Studies in *Indian Seals and Sealings*, Delhi, 1985.

Hastings, James, *Encyclopaedia of Religion and Ethics*, Vols. I-IV, New York, 1959.

Havel, F.B., *Ideals of Indian Art*, London, 1911.

Hopkins, E.W, *Epic Mythology*, London, 1905, Reprint, Delhi.

——, *The Religions of India*, 1895.

Jaya, Appaswamy, *Indian Paintings on Glass*, New Delhi, 1980.

Jivananda Sagara, *Brahvaivarta Purāṇa*, Calcutta, 1888.

Jivananda Vidyasagara, *Liṅga Purāṇa*, Calcutta, 1885.

John Campbell Oman, *The Mystics, Ascetics, and Saints of India*, 1903.

Kale, M.R., Ed., *Meghadūta* by Kālidāsa with Mallināthа's commentary, Bombay, 1926.

Kane, P.V., *History of Dharmaśāstra*, III, Poona, 1946.

——, *Taittarīya Saṁhitā* as quoted in *History of Dharmaśāstra*, III, Poona, 1946.

——, *Vājasneyī Saṁhita* as quoted in *History of Dharmaśāstra*, III, Poona, 1946.

——, *Gorakh Saṁhitā* as quoted in *History of Dharmaśāstra*, *III*, Poona, 1946.

——, *Baudhyāyana Dharmaśāstra* as quoted in *History of Dharmaśāstra*, III, Poona, 1946.

——, *Baudhyāyana Gṛhya Śeṣa-Sūtra* as quoted in *History of Dharmaśāstra*, III, *Poona*, 1946.

——; *Baudhyāyana Vaijvepya Gṛhya* Sutra as quoted in *History of Dharmaśāstra*, III, Poona, 1946.

——, *Bṛhannāradīya Purdna* as quoted in *History of Dharma-śāstra*, III, Poona, 1946.

——, *Kṛtya Kalpataru.*

——, *Mudgala Purāṇa* as quoted in *History-of* DharmaOstra, III, Poona, 1946.

Kennedy, J., *Hindu Mythology,* 1862.

——, *The Cult of Civilization of India,* Bombay, 1965.

Keith, *A.B., The Religion and Philosophy of Vedas and Upanisads,* Bombay, 1925.

Kosambi, D.D., *Myth and Reality*, Bombay, 1962.

Kramrisch, Stella, *Indian Sculpture,* London, 1933.

Krishnamurti, K., Ed. text and trans., *Dhvanyaloka* by Anandavardhana, Dharwar, 1974.

La, May, R., *The Culture of South East Asia,* London, 1954.

Lāla Baij Nath, R.B., *Hinduism, Ancient and Modern,* 1905.

Levy, Sylvain, *La Nepal*, Paris, 1905.

Linder, B., Ed.; *Kausītaki Brāhmaṇa,* Jena, 1887.

Macdonell, A.A., *Vedic Mythology,* Strassburg, 1897.

Majumdar, R.C., *Ancient Indian Colonies in the Far East,* Lahore, 1927.

Marian Edwardes and Lewis Spence, *Dictionary of Non-classical Mythology,* 1913.

Mario, Bassağli, *Paintings from Central Asia,* Geneva, 1963.

——, *Mathura Museum Catalogue.*

Martin Hang. Ed. and trans., *Aitreya Brahmana,* Bombay, 1863.

Max Mūller, F, *History of Ancient Literature,* 1859.

——, Ed., *Ṛgveda* Saṁhitā, with Sāyaṇa's commentary, 4 vols., London, 1890-92.

——, *Chips from a German Workshop* (4 vols.), 1868-1875.

——, *The Sacred 'Book of the East,* Oxford, 1910, Reprint Delhi, 1963.

——, (Ed.), Rgveda, *with commentery of Sāyaṇa,* London, 1849-1874.

Mishra, O.P., *Iconography of Saptamatrikas,* Delhi, 1989.

Mishra, Ram Nath, *Yaksa Cult and Iconography,* Delhi, 1981.

Monier Williams, *Religious Thought and Life in India,* 1883.

——, *Indian Epic Poetry,* 1863.

——, *Indian Wisdom,* 1875.

——, *Brahmanism and Hinduism,* 1887.

——, *Sanskrit English Dictionary,* Varanasi, 1966.

Moor, Edward, *Hindu Pantheon,* Reprint, Delhi, 1968.

Muir, J., *Original Sanskrit Texts,* 1870.

Murdoch, *Christian Literature Society's Handbooks.*

Murray Mitchell, J., *The Great Religions of India,* 1906.

Nagar, S.L., *Composite Deities in Indian Art,* New Delhi, 1988.

——, Śiva *in Indian Thought and Literature,* Delhi, 1991.

Nagendra Apte, *Matsya Purapa,* Poona, 1907.

——, *Nāradīya Purāṇa,* Poona, 1907.

——, *Nārasiṁha Purdna,* Poona, 1907.

Nandargikar, G.R., Ed., *Raghuvaṁśa* by Kālidāsa with the commentary of Mallinatha and others, Bombay, 1897.

Narayana Apte, *Brahma Purdna,* Poona, 1895.

Narayana Pillai, Ed., Avantisundarīkathā of Daṇḍin.

Narayana Pillai, Ed., *Daakumdracarita of Daṇḍin.*

Narayana Sastri, Godabole, Ed., *Taitirīya Brahmana with coin-mentary of Sāyaṇa,* Poona, 1898.

Pal. Pratapditya, *Art of Tibet,* London, 1983.

——, Composite form of Vasudeva and Lakṣmī, *Journal of Asiatic Society,* of Calcutta, Vol. IV. Panchanana Tarkaratna, Ed., *Mahābhārata,* with commetary of Nīlakaṇṭha, Calcutta- Saka Sam., 1826.

Pandey, Ram Tej, *Bhāgavata Purāṇa,* Varanasi, 1962.

Indian Images of Gods and Goddesses

Pandey, Ram Tirath, *Dēvī Bhāgavata Purāṇa,* Varanasi, 1966.

Pandit, S.P., Ed., *Atharvaveda, with commentary* of *Sāyana,* Bombay, 1895-1898.

Paranavitana, S. and Godakumbura, C.E., Ed., *Jānakiharaṇa* by Kumāradāsa, Ceylon, 1967.

Parasurama Lakshmana Vaida, Ed., *Harivaṁśa Purāṇa* Poona, 1963.

Penzer, N.M., *The Ocean of Stories,* London, 1924.

Prabha Chandra, *Historical Mahākāvyas,* Delhi., 1976.

Pushpendra Kumar, *Śiva Purāṇa,* Delhi, 1981.

Quakenbos, G.K., *The Sanskrit Poems of Mayūra,* New York, 1917.

Radhakrishan, *S., Bhagavadgītā,* George Allen and Urwin, London, 1958.

——, *The Principal Upaniṣads,* George Allen and Urwin, London, 1953.

——, *Indian Philosophy,* 2 vols. George Allen and Urwin, London, 1953.

Raghubir and Lokesa Chandra, *Jaiminīya Brāhmaṇa,* Nagpur, 1954.

Raghunath Sing, *Rājaraṅgini of Kalhaṇa,* Varanasi, 1970.

Ramanakrishnakavi, M. and Ramaswami Sastri, K.S., Ed., *Nātyaśāstras,* by Bharata text, commentary of Abhinavagupta 4 vols., Gaekwad Oriental Series 1956; text trans. M.M. Ghosh 2 vols. Calcutta 1967, 1961.

Rao, T.A., Gopinatha, Elements of *Hindu Iconography,* Vol. I, Pt. I, (Reprint, Delhi, 1968).

Rapson, E.J., *Ancient India,* Cambridge, 1916.

Ray, Nihar Ranjan, *Brahmanical Gods in Burma,* Rangoon, 1932.

Robson, J., *Hinduism and Christianity,* 1905.

Romesh Dutt, *The Epic of Ancient India*, 1899.

Sachau; E.C., Albirunis India, Delhi, 1964.

Sarasvati, S.K., *Survey of Indian Sculpture*, Calcutta, 1957.

Sarkar, D.C., *Select Inscriptions*, Vol. II, Delhi, 1983.

Sarma, I.K., Buddhist *Monuments in China and* South East Asia, Delhi, 1985.

Sastri, K. Krishna, *South Indian Images of Gods and Goddesses*, Madras, 1916.

Sastri, Kuppuswami, M.M.S., Ed., *Rāmāyaṇa* by Vālmīki, Madras, 1916.

Sastri, Laksman, M.M., Ed., *Nyāyakusumañjali* by Udyana, with the commentaries of Ruchidatta and Vardhamānopadhyāya, Banaras, 1912.

Shah, Priyabala, see *Viṣṇudharmottara.*

Sharma, B.N., *Vinayaka*, New Delhi; 1972.

Singh, Rajendra Prasad, *Chausaṭha Yoginiyan Evam Unke Mandir* (Hindi), Delhi, 1990.

Śivaramamurti, C., Chitsūtra of the *Viṣṇudharmottara*, Delhi, 1978.

——, *Sources of History Illumined* by Literature, Delhi, 1979.

——, *Approach to Nature in Indian Art and Thought*, Delhi, 1980.

——, *Gaṅga*, Orient Longmans, Delhi, 1977.

——, *Ṛṣis in Art and Literature*, New Delhi, 1981.

——, *Ethical Fragrance in Indian Art and Literature*, Delhi, 1980.

——, *Some Aspects of Indian Culture*, Delhi, 1969.

——, *Expressive Quality of Literary Flavour in Art*, Dharwar, 1974.

——, *Amarāvati Sculptures in the Madras Government Museum*, Madras, 1942.

——, *Satarudrīya, Vibhūti* of Śiva's Iconography, Delhi, 1976.

——, *Le Art en Inde*, Mazenod, Paris, 1974.

——, *La Sculpture de Rorobudur*, Paris, 1960.

Sleeman, *W.H., Rambles and Recollections,* (2 vols.), 1843.

Smith, V.A., *Catalogue of Coins in Indian Meseum,* Calcutta, (Reprint), Delhi, 1972.

Stacher, J., *The Arsenal,* 1910.

Subramanian, N.S., *Encyclopaedia of Upanisads,* Bangalore, 1985.

Sukla, D.N., Vastu Śaśtra.

Sukla, D.N. and Gopinatha Rao, Kharotragacha-granthamālā by Acharya Dinakra.

Sukla, D.N. and Gopinatha Rao, Pratiṣṭha Vidhi.

Thakur, Amresvara, Ed., *Rāmāyaṇa of Vālmīki,* with commentary of Lokanath, Calcutta, 1929.

Thaphyal, K.K., *Studies in Ancient Indian Seal,* Lucknow, 1972.

Tylor, B. (Ed.), *Primitive Culture,* (2 vols.), 1891.

Veronica, Ions, *Indian Mythology,* England, 1967.

Vimalananda, Swami, text trans., *Mahānārāyaṇopaniṣad,* Rāma-Kṛṣna Math, Madras, 1968.

Vogel, J.Ph., *Antiquities of Chamba State,* I, ASI, Memoir No. 78, Calcutta.

——, La Sculpture de Mathūrā, Ars Asiatica, Paris, 1930.

——, Woman and Tree or Sālabhañjikā in Indian Literature and Art, Acta Orientatia, 7, London, 1929.

——, Indian Serpent Lore or the Nāgas in Indian Legend and, Art.

Ward, W., *A View of the History, Literature and Religion of the Hindus,* 1863.

Weber, A., Ed., *Vājasaneyī Saṁhitā* with the commentary of Mahīdhara.

Wilkins, W.J., *Hindu Mythology,* 1900.

Wilson, H.H., *Essays on the Religions of the Hindus,* 1862.

Wilson, H.H., *Viṣṇu Purāṇa* Bombay, 1902.

Winternitz, M., *History of Indian Literature,* Calcutta, 1927.

Zimmer, H., *Myths and Symbols in Indian Art Civilization,* New York, 1972.

——, *The Art of Indian Asia,* New York, 1955.

Index

C

D

F

G

H

I

J

K

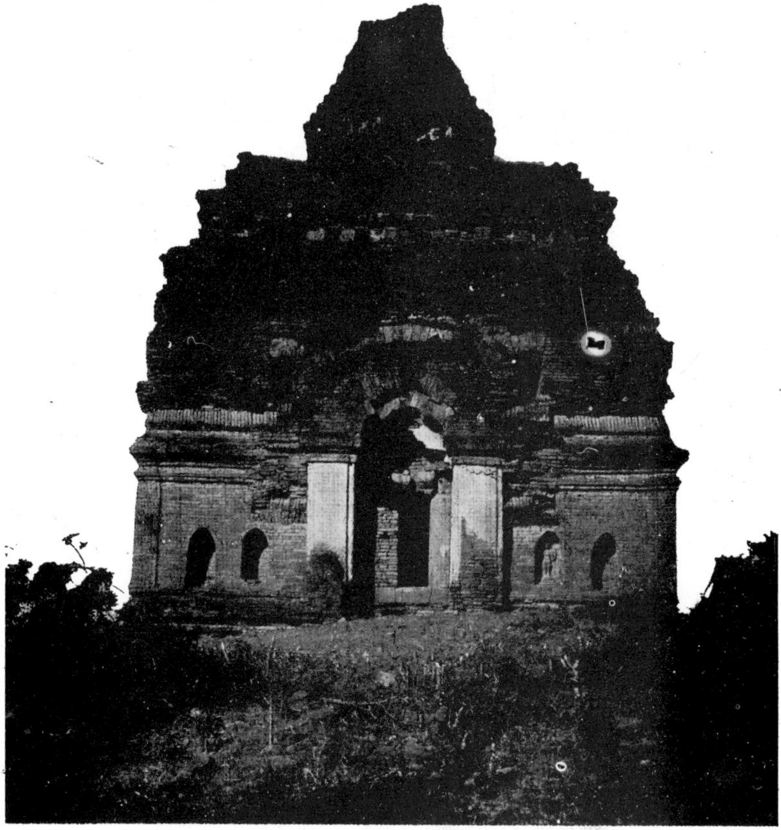

Pl. 1 *Nāt-hlaung kyaung,* the only ancient Brahmanical temple extant in Burma, Pagan; now in good state of preservation. It is a Viṣṇuite temple which had originally sheltered in its niches images of the ten *avatāras of Viṣṇu*. Some of the niches are now empty. C. 10th century A.D. (Courtesy: Archaeological Survey, Burma).

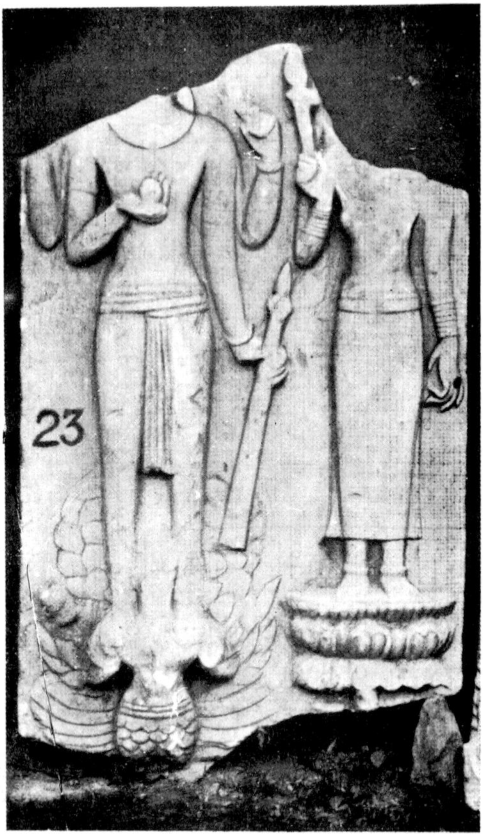

Pl. 2 *Viṣṇu* and *Lakṣmī* standing: *Phoongyi kyaung* shed, Hmawza, Prome; well-preserved, though mutilated at the top and base. C. 8th century A.D.

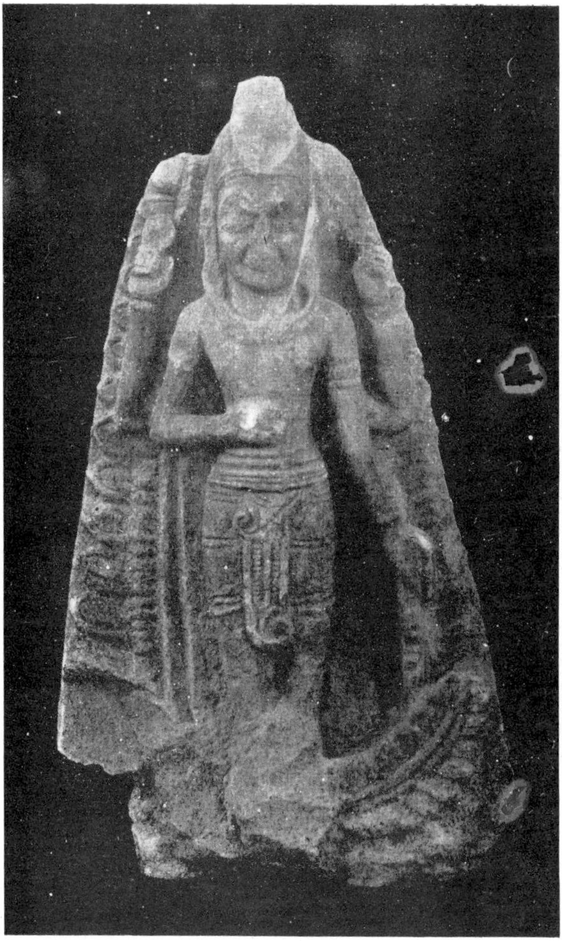

Pl. 3 *Viṣṇu* standing on *Garuḍa : Phoongyi kyaung* shed, Hmawza, Prome; slightly mutilated at the top and base. C. 8th century A.D. (Courtesy: Archaeological Survey, Burma).

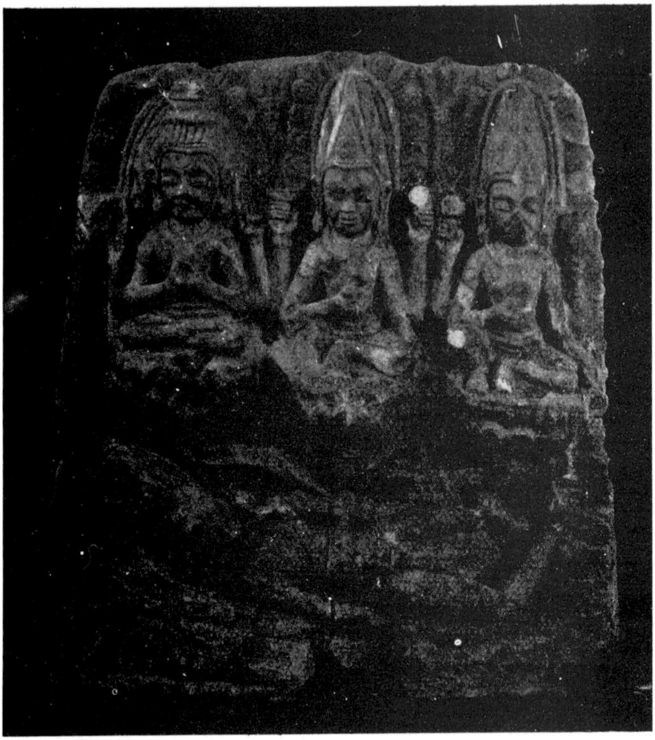

Pl. 4 *Viṣṇu* lying on the serpent *Ananta : Phoongyi kyaung* shed, Hmawza, Prome; very badly corroded, lower-half broken into two. C. 8th century A.D. (Courtesy: Archaeological Survey, Burma).

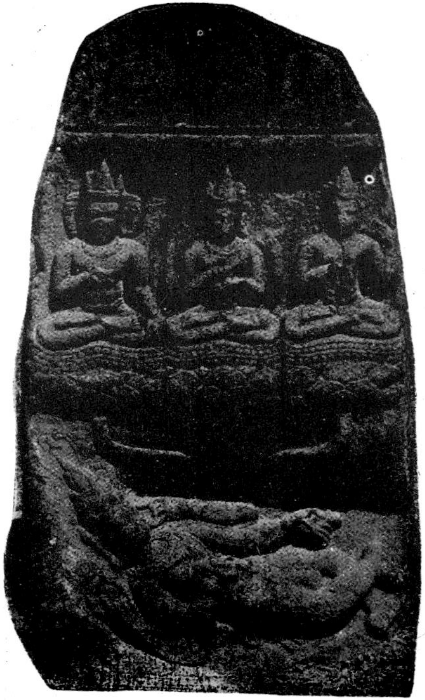

Pl. 5 *Viṣṇu* lying on the serpent *Ananta;* originally discovered at Thātoñ; now in the Government Museum, Rangoon: well preserved. C. 9th century A.D. (Courtesy: Archaeological Survey, Burma).

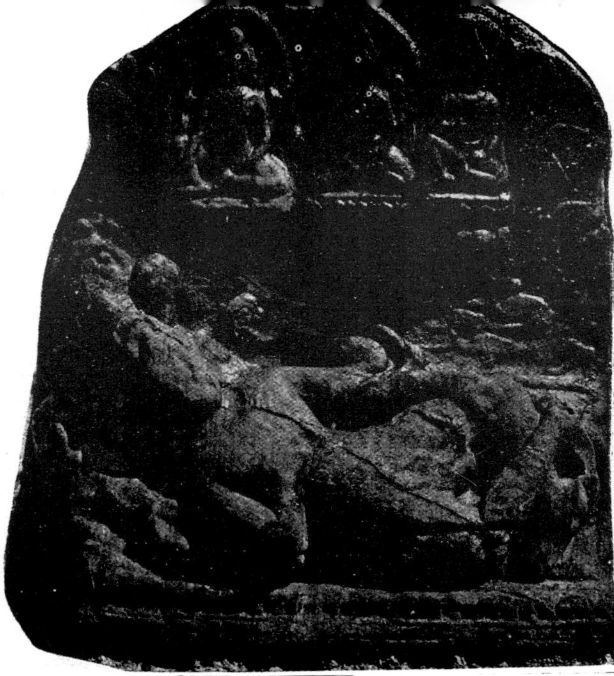

Pl. 6 *Viṣṇu* lying on the serpent *Ananta;* originally discovered at Thātoñ; now in the Government Museum, Rangoon; broken into several pieces which are all very sadly corroded. C. 9th century A.D. (Courtesy. Archaeological Survey, Burma).

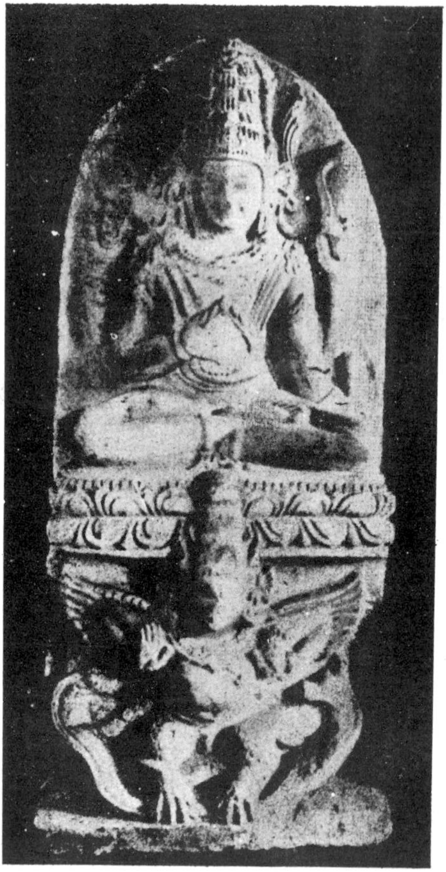

Pl. 7 *Viṣṇu* seated on *Garuḍa:* the main deity of the *Nāt-hlaung kyaung,* Pagan; now in the Berlin Museum, well preserved. *C.* 10th-11th century A.D. (Courtesy: Berlin Museum).

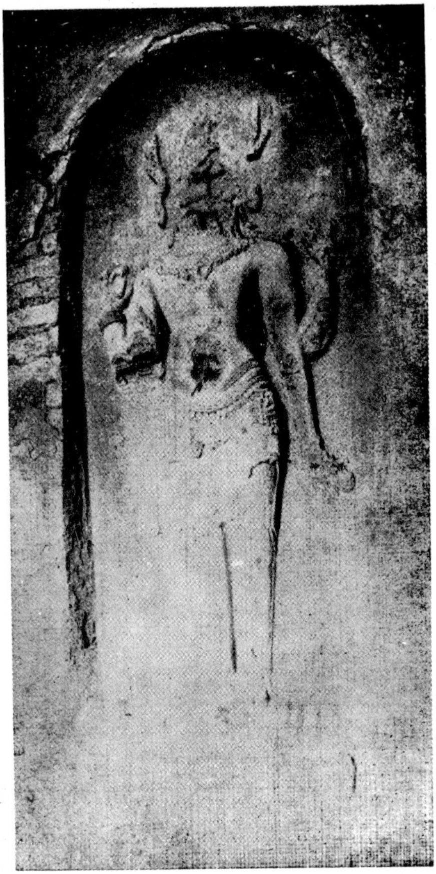

Pl. 8 Four-handed *Viṣṇu* standing; one of the four very badly mutilated images of standing *Viṣṇu* on the four sides of the central obelisk of the *Nāt-hlaung* temple, Pagan. C. 10th-11th century A.D. (Courtesy: Archaeological Survey, Burma).

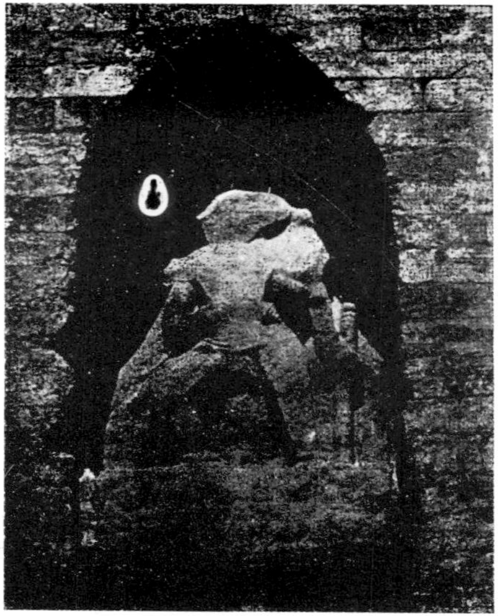

Pl. 9 *Varāha avatīra of Viṣṇu* : in an outer niche of the *Nāt-hlaung* temple, Pagan: very badly defaced. C. 10th-11th century A.D. (Courtesy: Archaeological Survey, Burma).

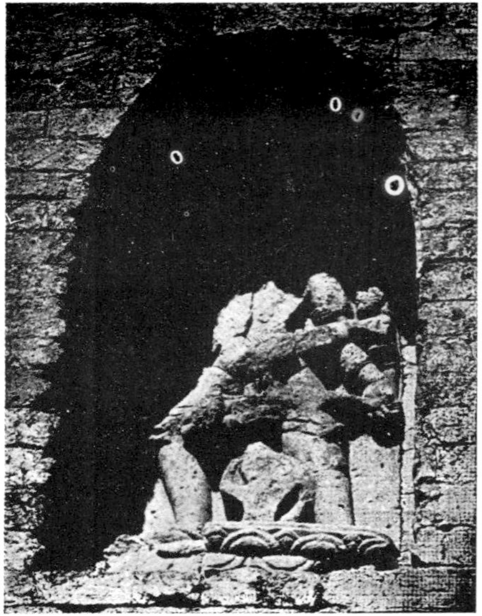

Pl. 10 *Narasiṁha avatāra of Viṣṇu;* in an outer niche of the *Nāt-hlaung* temple, Pagan: very badly defaced. C. 10th-11th century A.D. (Courtesy: Archaeological Survey, Burma).

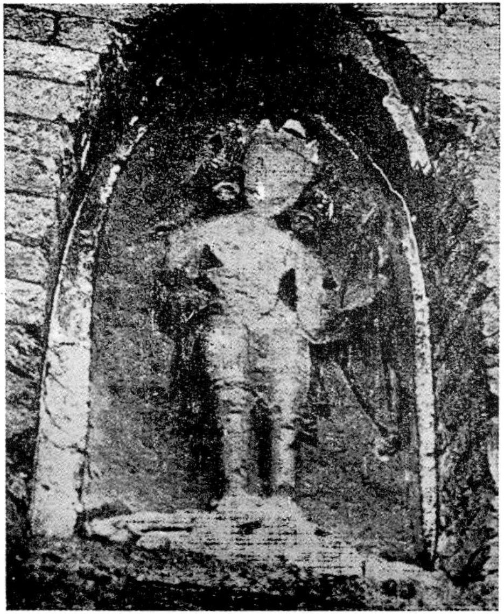

Pl. 11 *Rāmacandra avatāra* of *Viṣṇu;* in an outer niche of the *Nāt-hlaung* temple, Pagan: very badly defaced. *C.* 10th-11th century A.D. (Courtesy: Archaeological Survey, Burma).

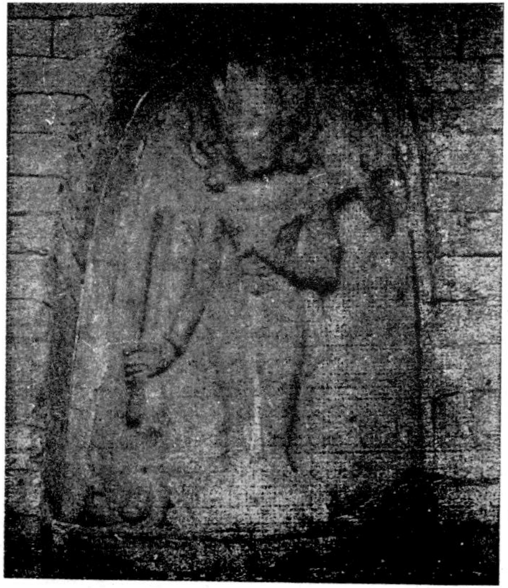

Pl. 12 *Paraśurāma avatāra* of *Viṣṇu* : in an outer niche of the *Nāt-hlaung* temple, Pagan: very badly defaced and corroded. *C.* 10th-11th century A.D. (Courtesy: Archaeological Survey, Burma).

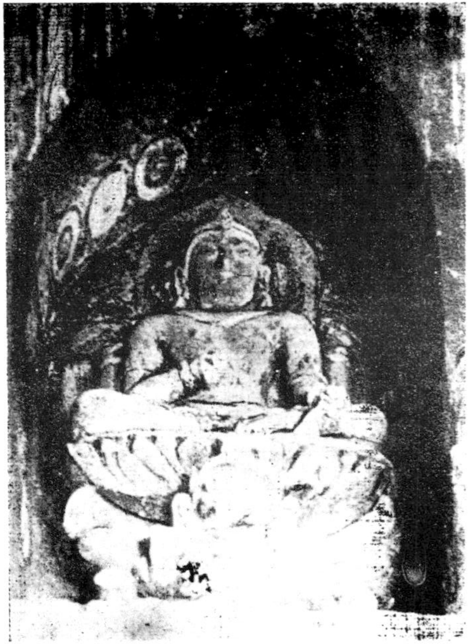

Pl. 13 *Buddha avatāra of Viṣṇu;* in one of the two niches above the main sanctum of the *Nat-hlaung* temple, the other niche is empty: slightly damaged, difficult to be photographed. C. 10th-11th century A.D. (Courtesy: Archaeological Survey, Burma).

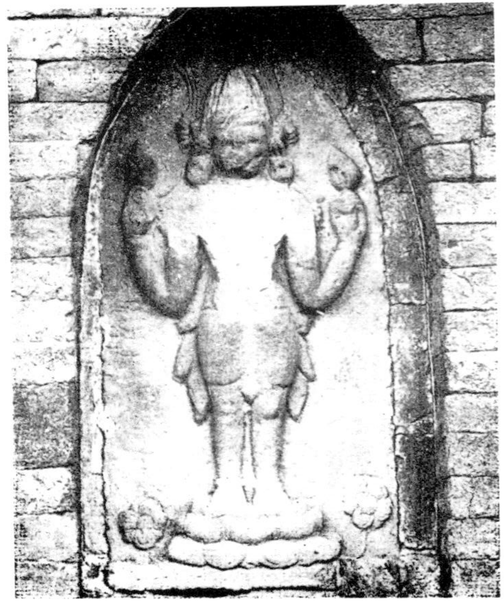

Pl. 14 *Sūrya* standing on a lotus; in an outer niche if the *Nāt-hlaung* temple, Pagan : portions of the body and face badly corroded. C. 10th-11th century A.D. (Courtesy: Archaeological Survey, Burma).

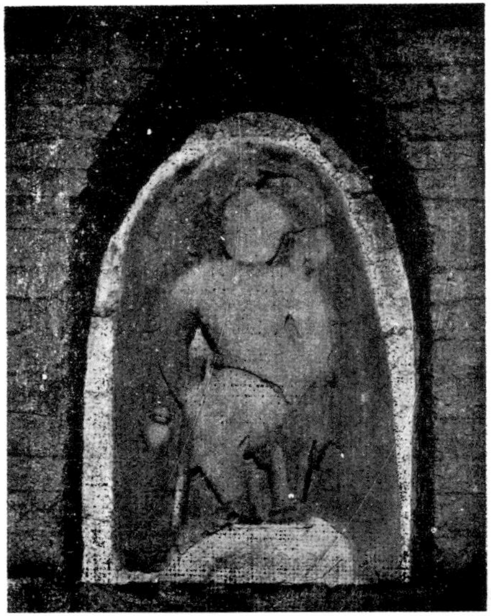

Pl. 15 *Vāmana avatāra* of *Viṣṇu;* in an outer niche of the *Nāt-hlaung* temple: very badly defaced. C. 10th-11th century A.D. (Courtesy: Archaeological Survey, Burma).

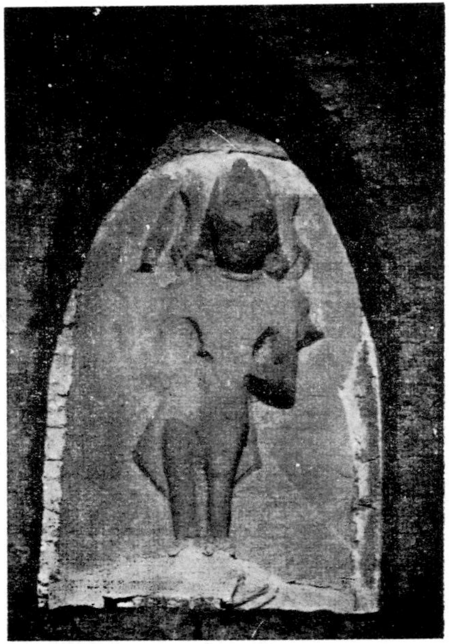

Pl. 16 *Kalki avatāra* of *Viṣṇu;* in an outer niche of the *Nāt hlaung* temple, Pagan: portions of the body badly mutilated. C. 10th-11th century A.D. (Courtesy: Archaeological Survey, Burma).

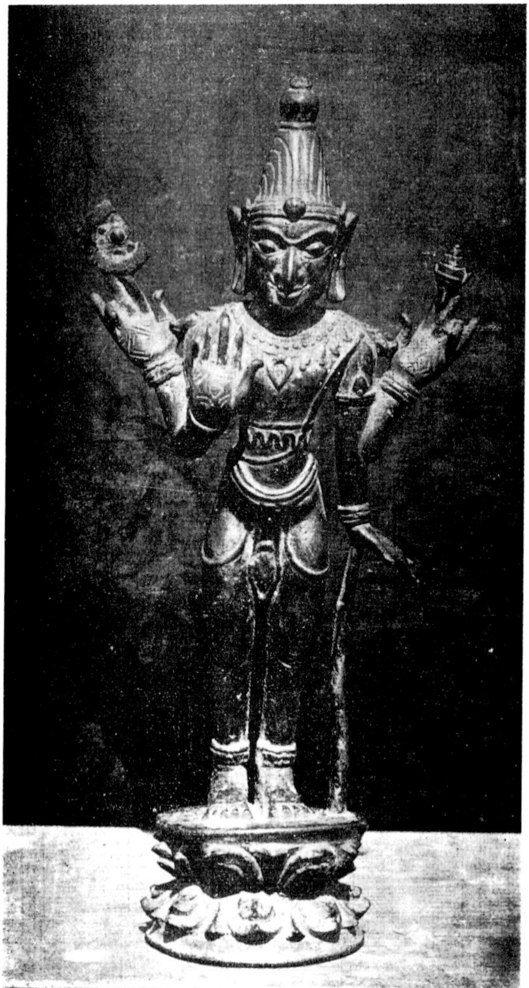

Pl. 17 Four-handed *Viṣṇu* standing on lotus pedestal; originally discovered at Myinkaba, now in the Ananda Museum, Pagan: bronze, well-preserved. C. 13th-14th century A.D. (Courtesy: Archaeological Survey, Burma).

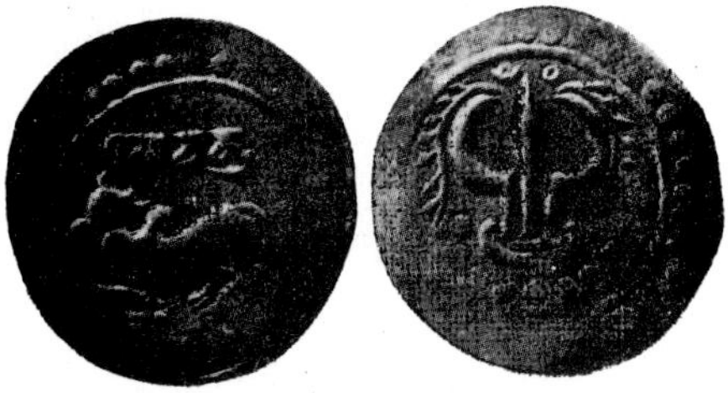

a

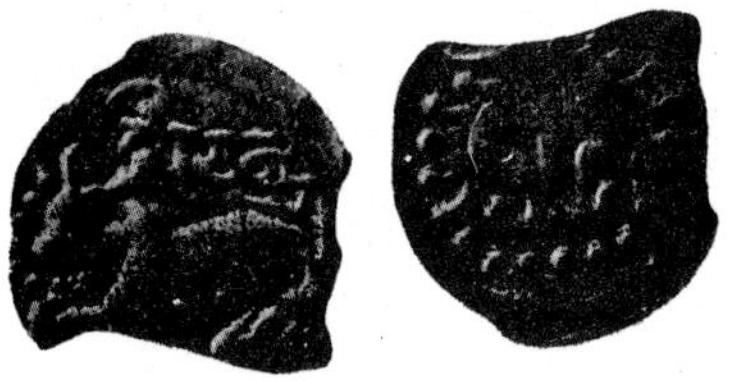

b

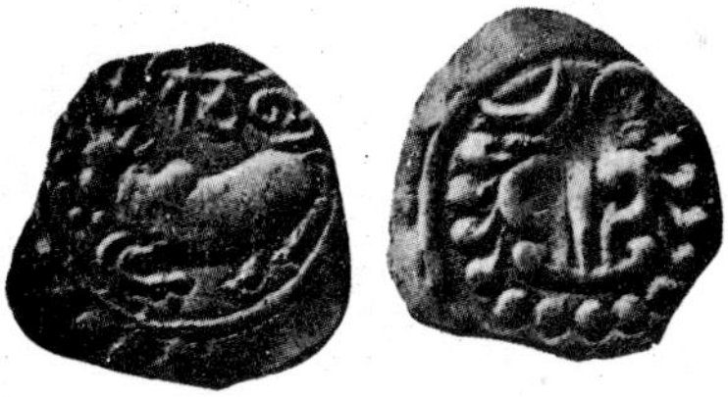

c

Pl. 18 Śaivite coins bearing obverse and reverse legends of bull and trident respectively, belonging to the ancient *Candra* dynasty of kings of Arakan; inscribed in *nāgarī* characters of the 9th-11th century A.D. (Phayre: Coins of Arakan, Pegu and Burma, Plate II, nos. 1, 4, 8; pp. 28-29).

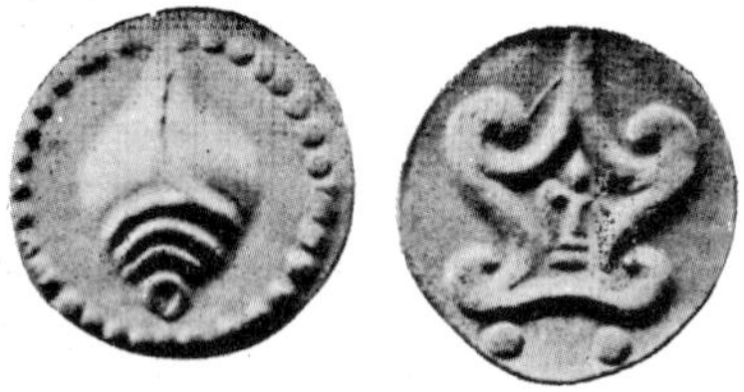

a

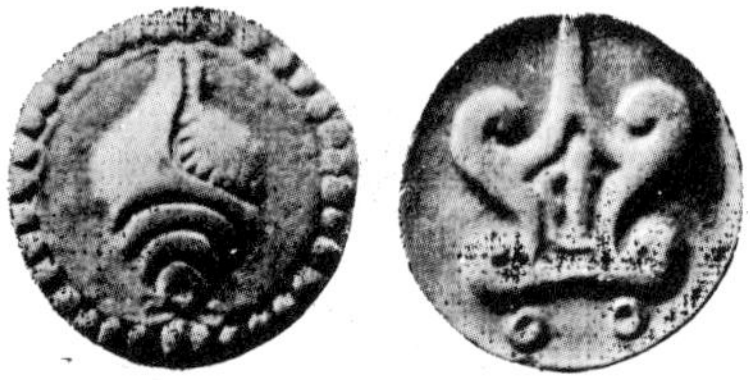

b

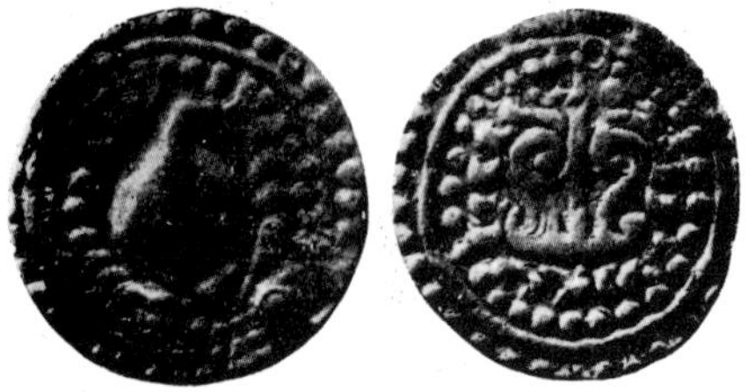

c

Pl. 19 Coins bearing obverse and reverse legends of *Viṣṇuite* conch-shell and Śaivite trident respectively, belonging probably to the ancient *Candra* dynasty of kings of Arakan. (Phayre : Coins of Arakan, Pegu and Burma, plate V, nos. 6 and 7 and plate II, no. 10; p. 33 and p. 29).

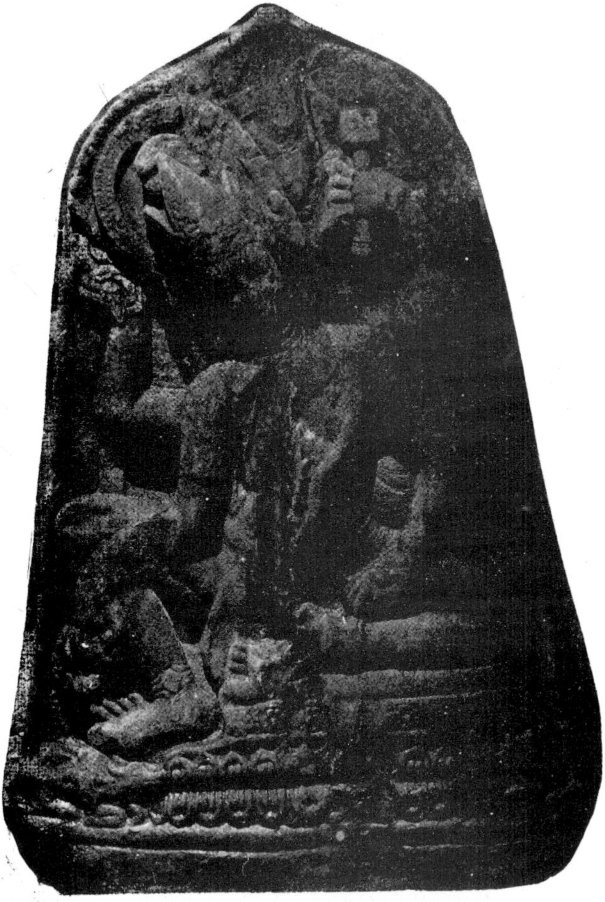

Pl. 20 *Śiva* and *Pārvatī* seated: originally discovered at Thātoñ now in the Government Museum, Rangoon: well preserved, though slightly mutilated. C. 9th century A.D. (Courtesy Archaeological Survey, Burma).

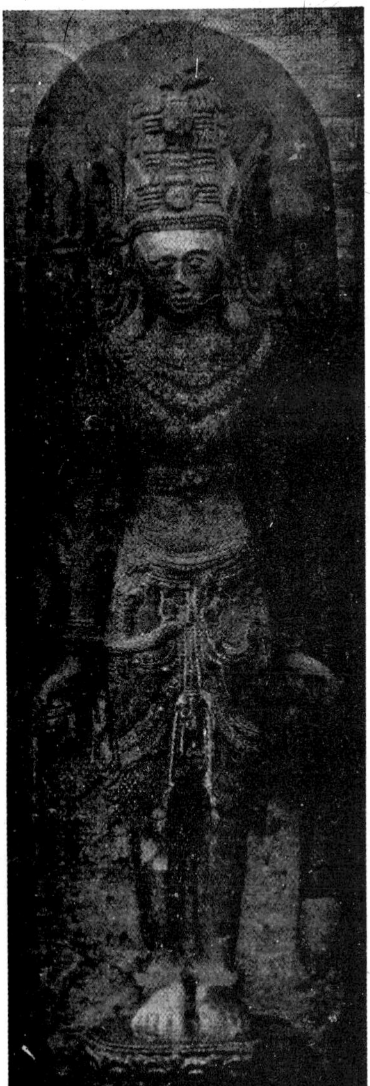

Pl. 21 *Śiva* standing: originally discovered amidst the debris of ruins within the *Nāt-hlaung* temple, Pagan; now in the Ananda Museum: well preserved. C. 13th century A.D. (Courtesy : Archaeological Survey, Burma).

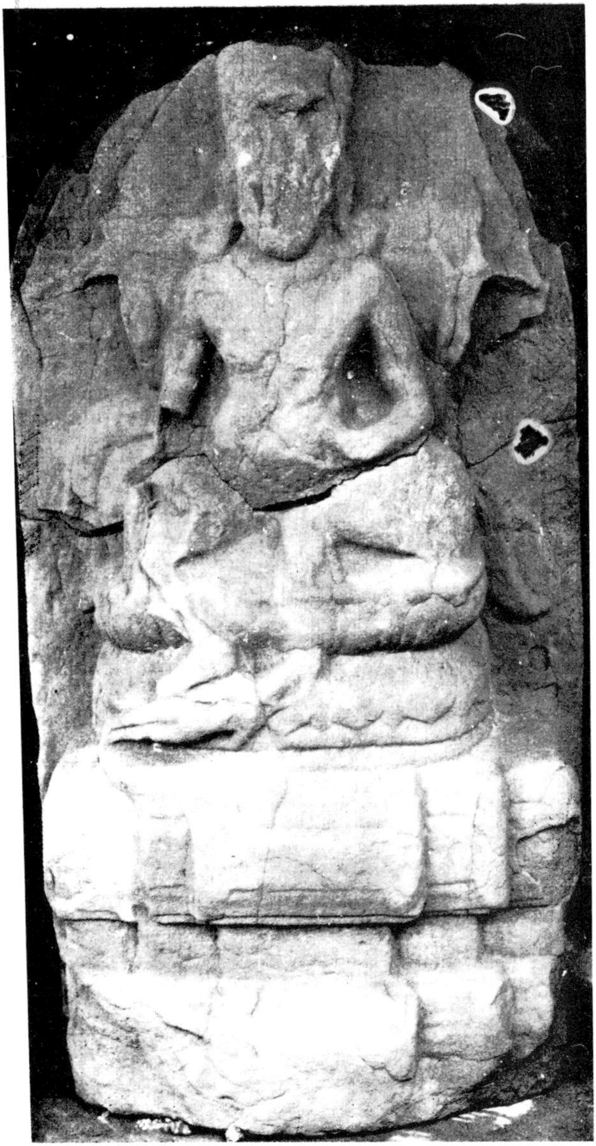

Pl. 22 *Śiva* seated in *rāja-līlā* : originally discovered near *Shwe-ōnhmin* monastery at Myinpagan; now in the Ananda Museum, Pagan: very badly mutilated. C. 10th-11th century A.D. (Courtesy : Archaeological Survey, Burma).

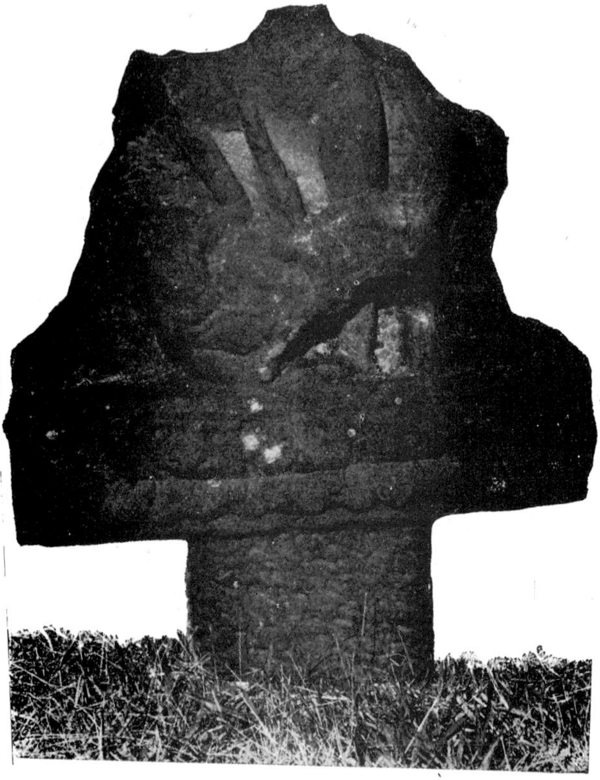

Pl. 23 *Devī* slaying the *Mahiṣāsura* (buffalo-demon); originally discovered at Wesali, Arakan; now at the office of the Honorary Archaeological Officer, Arakan : upper portion and sides of slab entirely broken off, very badly corroded. C. 6th-7th century A.D. (Courtesy: Archaeological Survey, Burma).

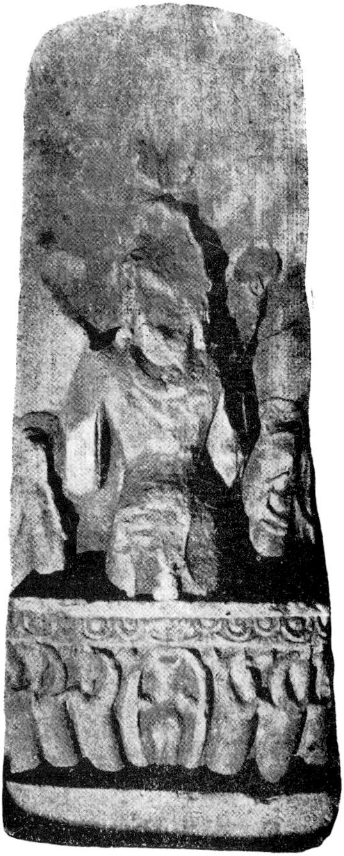

Pl. 24 *Sūrya* driving a chariot drawn by seven horses originally discovered at Mrohaung, Arakan; now at the office of the Honorary Archaeological Officer, Arakan : very badly mutilated. *C.* 6th 7th century A.D. (Courtesy: Archaeological Survey, Burma).

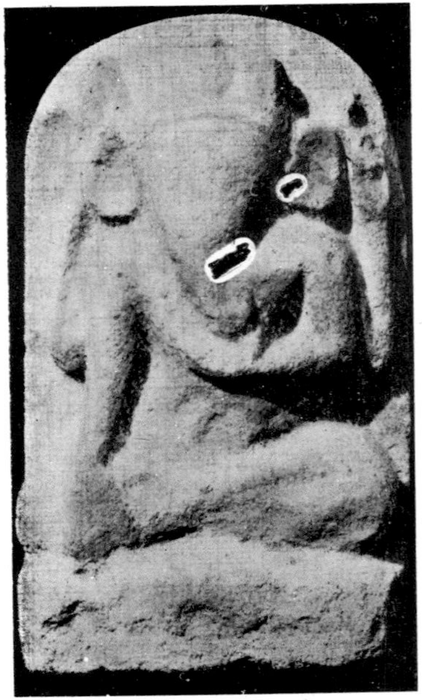

Pl. 25 *Gaṇeśa* seated in *padmāsana*, Ananda Museum, Pagan : very badly mutilated. C. 11th-12th century A.D. (Courtesy: Archaeological Survey, Burma).

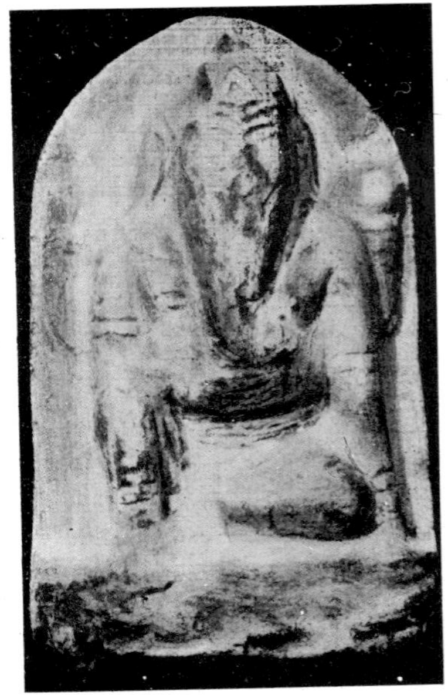

Pl. 26 *Gaṇeśa* seated in *padmāsana*, Ananda Museum, Pagan : very badly weathered. C. 12th-13th century A.D. (Courtesy: Archaeological Survey, Burma).

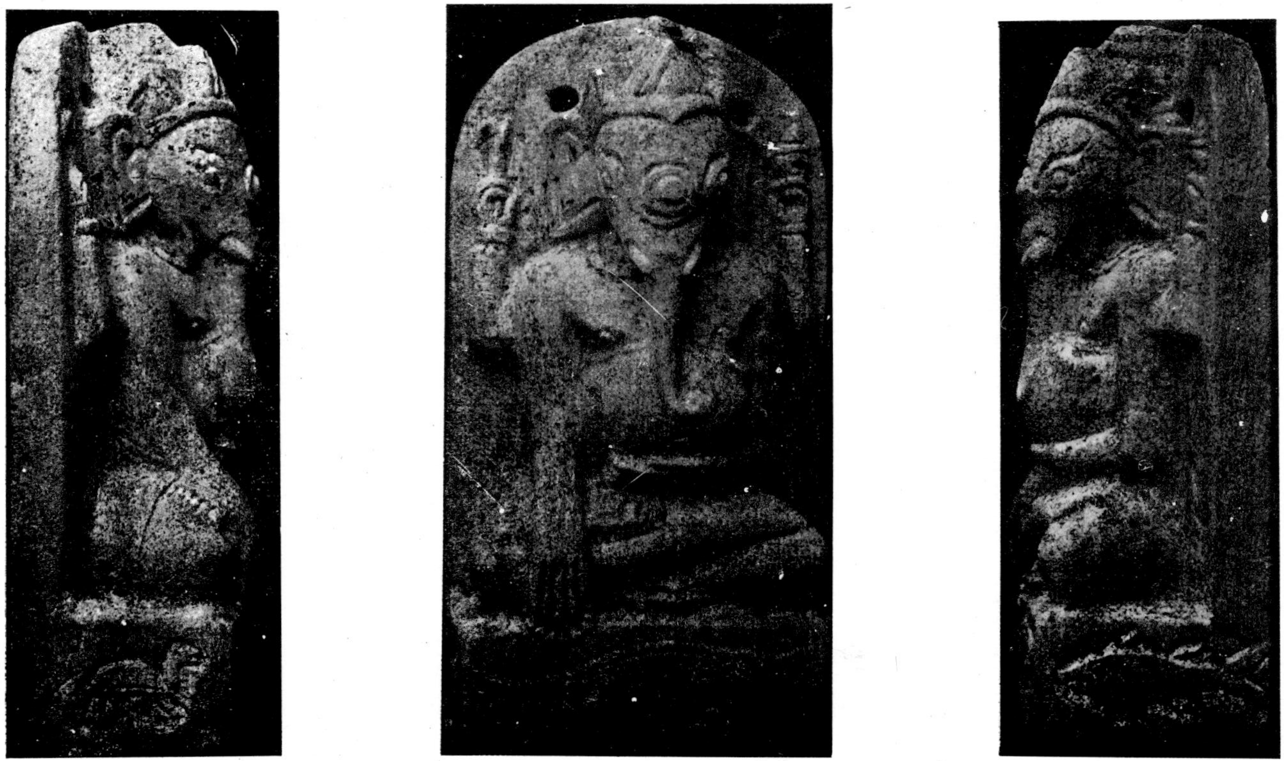

a *b* *c*

Pl. 27 *Gaṇeśa* seated on a pedestal showing on its fate a crocodile, and on the right and left a tortoise and a fish respectively: originally found at Pagan; now at the office of the Archaeological Survey, Mandalay: good state of preservation. C. 13th-14th century A.D. (Courtesy: Archaeological Survey, Burma).

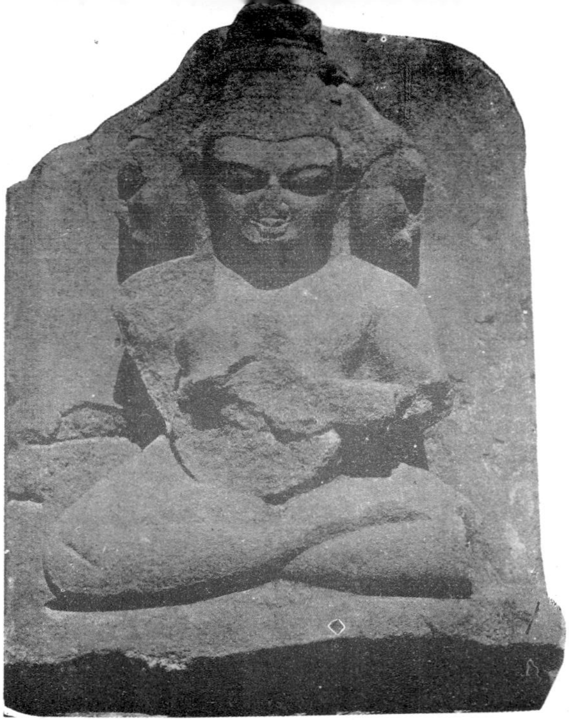

l. 28 *Brahmā* seated in *padmāsana*, Ananda Museum, Pagan: portions of the body, broken off. *C.* 9th-10th century A.D. (Courtesy: Archaeological Survey, Burma).

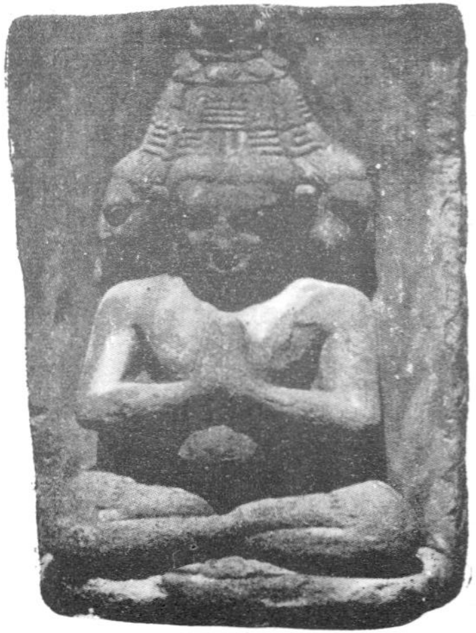

Pl. 29 *Brahmā* seated in *padmāsana*, Government Museum, Rangoon: well-preserved. *C.* 12th century A.D. (Courtesy: Archaeological Survey, Burma).

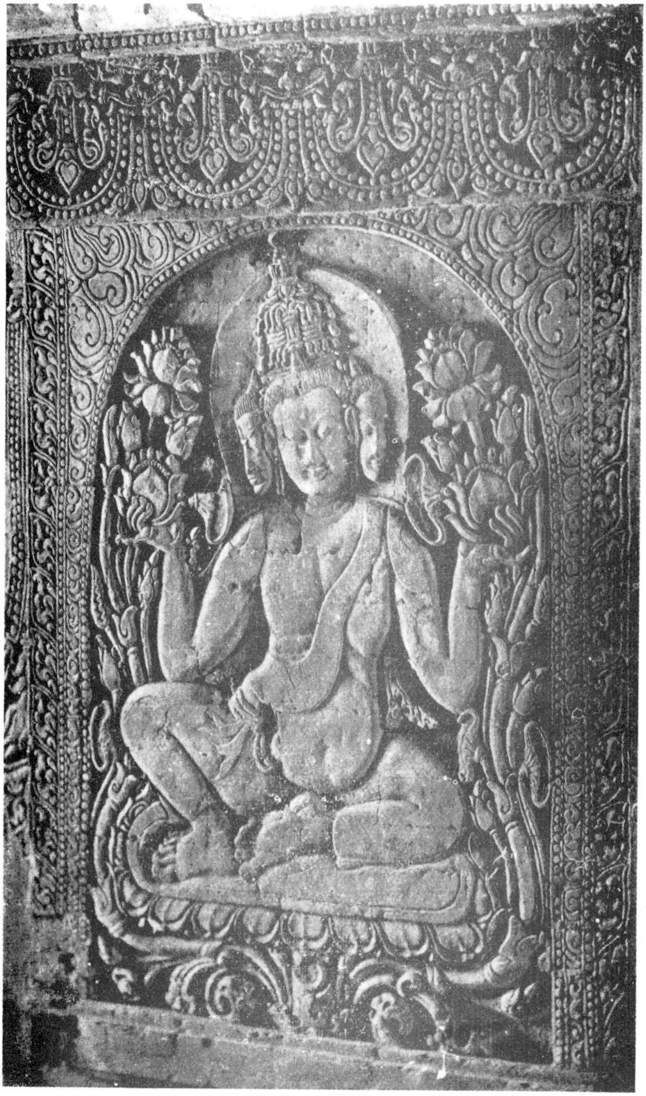

Pl. 30 *Brahmā* seated in *līlāsana, Nanpaya* temple, Myinpagan, Pagan; very well-preserved. C. 11th century A.D. (Courtesy: Archaeological Survey, Burma).